HERITAGE AUCTION GALLERIES PROUDLY PRESENTS

PLATINUM N

MW01233000

KUTASI COLLECTION
F.U.N. SIGNATURE AUCTION #422
JANUARY 3-6, 2007 • ORLANDO, FLORIDA

MAIN EXHIBITION OF LOTS

Orange County Convention Center • North/South Building • Room 220 D, E, F
9860 Universal Blvd • Orlando, FL 32819

Monday, January 1st .... 9 AM-7 PM ET		Thursday, January 4th .... 8 AM-7 PM ET
Tuesday, January 2nd .... 8 AM-7 PM ET		Friday, January 5th .... 8 AM-7 PM ET
Wednesday, January 3rd .... 8 AM-7 PM ET		Saturday, January 6th .... 8 AM-5 PM ET

PUBLIC, INTERNET AND MAIL BID AUCTION #422

Orange County Convention Center • North/South Building; Room 230 A, B
9860 Universal Blvd • Orlando, FL 32819

Session 1 .... Wednesday, January 3 .... 2 PM ET
Session 2 ...... (Platinum Night I) .... Wednesday, January 3 .... Dinner @ 5 PM ET; Auction @ 6 PM ET
Session 3 ...... (Patterns)................................... Wednesday, January 3 .... Approx 8:30 PM ET
Session 4 .... Thursday, January 4 .... 9:30 AM ET
Session 5 .... Thursday, January 4 .... 2 PM ET
Session 6 ...... (Dr. Loewinger Collection) ...... Thursday, January 4 .... Dinner @ 6 PM ET; Auction @ 7 PM ET
Session 7 .... (Kutasi Collection).................... Thursday, January 4 .... Approx 8 PM ET...Lots 3150-3310
Session 8 .... (Platinum Night II) .... Thursday, January 4 .... Approx 9 PM ET
Session 9 .... Friday, January 5 .... 9 AM ET
Session 10 .... Friday, January 5 .... 2 PM ET
Session 11 .... Friday, January 5 .... 5 PM ET
Session 12 .... Saturday, January 6 .... 9:30 AM ET
Session 13 .... Saturday, January 6 .... 1 PM ET
Session 14 .... Saturday, January 6 .... 5 PM ET

Lots are generally sold at the approximate rate of 200 per hour, but it is not uncommon to sell 150 lots or 300 lots in any given hour. Please plan accordingly so that you don't miss the items you are bidding on.

This auction is subject to a 15% Buyer's Premium.

The World's #1 Numismatic Auctioneer

HERITAGE
Auction Galleries

3500 Maple Avenue, 17th Floor, Dallas, Texas 75219-3941
214-528-3500 • 800-US COINS (872-6467)

LOT SETTLEMENT AND PICKUP:

Thurs.-Sat., Jan. 4-6..... 10 AM – 1 PM
Sun., Jan. 7 .... 9 AM – 12 PM
(By appointment only)

Direct Client Service Line: Toll Free 1-866-835-3243 • e-mail: **Bid@HA.com**

View full-color images at **HA.com/Coins**

Auctioneer: Samuel W. Foose AU3244
Heritage Numismatic Auctions, Inc: AB0000665

Cataloged by Mark Van Winkle, Chief Cataloger;
Brian Koller, Catalog Production Manager; Mark Borckardt, Senior Cataloger;
Jon Amato, John Beety, Bill Fivaz, Stewart Huckaby, Greg Lauderdale, Bruce Lorich, David W. Perkins, John Salyer

Photography and Imaging by Jody Garver, Chief Photographer;
Leticia Crawford, Piper Crawley, Lucas Garritson, Thea Klaas, Lori McKay,
Deign Rook, Tony Webb, Jason Young,

Production and design by Cindy Brenner, Cathy Hadd, Katie Brown, Susan Jung

FAX BIDS TO:
214-443-8425

FAX DEADLINE:
Tues., Jan. 2, Noon CT

INTERNET BIDDING:
Closes at 10 PM CT
before the session
on sale

Auction
Results

Available Immediately
at our website:
HA.com/Coins

AUCTION #422

5866

Steve Ivy
CEO
Co-Chairman
of the Board

Jim Halperin
Co-Chairman
of the Board

Greg Rohan
President

Paul Minshull
Chief Operating
Officer

HERITAGE AUCTION GALLERIES

Dear FUN Bidder,

Welcome to the F.U.N. 2007 convention, and our Signature and Platinum Night sessions being held January 3-6, 2007 in Orlando – the "Auction of the Century!" This special Platinum Night catalog is dedicated to the important Kutasi Collection, and is one of five catalogs that comprise Platinum Nights. Heritage Auction Galleries, the Official Auctioneer of the Florida United Numismatists, is proud to present this leading Registry collection, which is currently ranked:

#1 Current and #1 All-Time $10 Indians
#1 Current and #2 All-Time Type 3 Liberty Double Eagles
#1 Current and #4 All-Time Saint-Gaudens Double Eagles

John Kutasi amassed one of the finest collections of 20th century gold ever assembled. A Los Angeles native, Mr. Kutasi received his B.S. in Business Administration from USC, and then worked in commodity futures trading. Ultimately, this entrepreneur acquired various business interests in the credit industry. A strong believer in gold, he began purchasing generic Saints, but his interest soon evolved into a deep appreciation for – and the pursuit of – rarer dates in $5 Indians, $10 Indians, and $20 Saints. Through his aggressive buying, constant upgrading, and close working relationship with dealers such as Heritage's Todd Imhof, he was able to assemble the magnificent coins presented here. Mr. Kutasi's achievement will be long remembered by numismatists for whom only the best is good enough.

We invite you to inspect and bid upon these important pieces of America's numismatic heritage. Opportunities to inspect and pursue so many superlative examples are rare indeed, and F.U.N. provides you with so many options; many gold specialists will be attending in person for these reasons.

Good luck with your bidding, whether you join us in Orlando, participate through the Internet at HA.com, or utilize our telephone, mail, fax, or agent options. If you can attend the "Auction of the Century" at F.U.N., please stop by lot viewing or our bourse table – we would love to chat with you.

Sincerely,

Greg Rohan
President

TERMS AND CONDITIONS OF AUCTION

Auctioneer and Auction:

1. This Auction is presented by Heritage Auction Galleries, a d/b/a/ of Heritage Auctions, Inc., or their affiliates Heritage Numismatic Auctions, Inc. or Currency Auctions of America, Inc., d/b/a as identified with the applicable licensing information on the title page of the catalog or on the HA.com Internet site (the "Auctioneer"). The Auction is conducted under these Terms and Conditions of Auction and applicable state and local law. Announcements and corrections from the podium and those made through the Terms and Conditions of Auctions appearing on the Internet at HA.com supersede those in the printed catalog.

Buyer's Premium:

2. On bids placed through Heritage, a Buyer's Premium of fifteen percent (15%) will be added to the successful hammer price bid on lots in Coin and Currency auctions, or nineteen and one-half percent (19.5%) on lots in all other auctions. If your bid is placed through eBay Live, a Buyer's Premium equal to the normal Buyer's Premium plus an additional five percent (5%) of the hammer price will be added to the successful bid up to a maximum Buyer's Premium of Twenty Two and one-half percent (22.5%). There is a minimum Buyer's Premium of $9.00 per lot. In Gallery Auctions only, a ten percent (10%) handling fee is applied to all lots based upon the total of the hammer price plus the 15% Buyer's Premium.

Auction Venues:

3. The following Auctions are conducted solely on the Internet: Heritage Weekly Internet Coin, Currency, Comics, and Vintage Movie Poster Auctions; Heritage Monthly Internet Sports and Marketplace Auctions; OnLine Sessions. Signature Auctions and Grand Format Auctions accept bids on the Internet first, followed by a floor bidding session; bids may be placed prior to the floor bidding session by Internet, telephone, fax, or mail.

Bidders:

4. Any person participating or registering for the Auction agrees to be bound by and accepts these Terms and Conditions of Auction ("Bidder(s)").

5. All Bidders must meet Auctioneer's qualifications to bid. Any Bidder who is not a customer in good standing of the Auctioneer may be disqualified at Auctioneer's sole option and will not be awarded lots. Such determination may be made by Auctioneer in its sole and unlimited discretion, at any time prior to, during, or even after the close of the Auction. Auctioneer reserves the right to exclude any person it deems in its sole opinion is disruptive to the Auction or is otherwise commercially unsuitable.

6. If an entity places a bid, then the person executing the bid on behalf of the entity agrees to personally guarantee payment for any successful bid.

Credit References:

7. Bidders who have not established credit with the Auctioneer must either furnish satisfactory credit information (including two collectibles-related business references) well in advance of the Auction or supply valid credit card information. Bids placed through our Interactive Internet program will only be accepted from pre-registered Bidders; Bidders who are not members of HA.com or affiliates should pre-register at least two business days before the first session to allow adequate time to contact references.

Bidding Options:

8. Bids in Signature Auctions or Grand Format Auctions may be placed as set forth in the printed catalog section entitled "Choose your bidding method." For auctions held solely on the Internet, see the alternatives on HA.com. Review at HA.com/common/howtobid.php.

9. Presentment of Bids: Non-Internet bids (including but not limited to podium, fax, phone and mail bids) are treated similar to floor bids in that they must be on-increment or at a half increment (called a cut bid). Any podium, fax, phone, or mail bids that do not conform to a full or half increment will be rounded up or down to the nearest full or half increment and this revised amount will be considered your high bid.

10. Auctioneer's Execution of Certain Bids. Auctioneer cannot be responsible for your errors in bidding, so carefully check that every bid is entered correctly. When identical mail or FAX bids are submitted, preference is given to the first received. To ensure the greatest accuracy, your written bids should be entered on the standard printed bid sheet and be received at Auctioneer's place of business at least two business days before the Auction start. Auctioneer is not responsible for executing mail bids or FAX bids received on or after the day the first lot is sold, nor Internet bids submitted after the published closing time; nor is Auctioneer responsible for proper execution of bids submitted by telephone, mail, FAX, e-mail, Internet, or in person once the Auction begins. Internet bids may not be withdrawn until your written request is received and acknowledged by Auctioneer (FAX: 214-443-8425); such requests must state the reason, and may constitute grounds for withdrawal of bidding privileges. Lots won by mail Bidders will not be delivered at the Auction unless prearranged.

11. Caveat as to Bid Increments. Bid increments (over the current bid level) determine the lowest amount you may bid on a particular lot. Bids greater than one increment over the current bid can be any whole dollar amount. It is possible under several circumstances for winning bids to be between increments, sometimes only $1 above the previous increment. Please see: "How can I lose by less than an increment?" on our website.

The following chart governs current bidding increments.

Current Bid	Bid Increment	Current Bid	Bid Increment
< $10	$1	$3,000 - $4,999	$250
$10 - $29	$2	$5,000 - $9,999	$500
$30 - $59	$3	$10,000 - $19,999	$1,000
$60 - $99	$5	$20,000 - $29,999	$2,000
$100 - $199	$10	$30,000 - $49,999	$2,500
$200 - $299	$20	$50,000 - $99,999	$5,000
$300 - $499	$25	$100,000 - $249,999	$10,000
$500 - $999	$50	$250,000 - $499,999	$25,000
$1,000 - $1,999	$100	$500,000 - $1,499,999	$50,000
$2,000 - $2,999	$200	> $1,500,000	$100,000

12. If Auctioneer calls for a full increment, a floor/phone bidder may request Auctioneer to accept a bid at half of the increment ("Cut Bid") which will be that bidders final bid; if the Auctioneer solicits bids other the expected increment, they will not be considered Cut Bids, and bidders accepting such increments may continue to participate.

Conducting the Auction:

13. Notice of the consignor's liberty to place reserve bids on his lots in the Auction is hereby made in accordance with Article 2 of the Texas Uniform Commercial Code. A reserve is an amount below which the lot will not sell. THE CONSIGNOR OF PROPERTY MAY PLACE WRITTEN RESERVE BIDS ON HIS LOTS IN ADVANCE OF THE AUCTION; ON SUCH LOTS, IF THE HAMMER PRICE DOES NOT MEET THE RESERVE, THE CONSIGNOR MAY PAY A REDUCED COMMISSION ON THOSE LOTS. Reserves are generally posted online several days prior to the Auction closing. Any successful bid placed by a consignor on his Property on the Auction floor or by telephone during the live session, or after the reserves for an Auction have been posted, will be considered an Unqualified Bid, and in such instances the consignor agrees to pay full Buyer's Premium and Seller's Commissions on any lot so repurchased.

14. The highest qualified Bidder shall be the buyer. In the event of any dispute between floor Bidders at a Signature Auction, Auctioneer may at his sole discretion reoffer the lot. Auctioneer's decision and declaration of the winning Bidder shall be final and binding upon all Bidders.

15. Auctioneer reserves the right to refuse to honor any bid or to limit the amount of any bid which, in his sole discretion, is not submitted in "Good Faith," or is not supported by satisfactory credit, numismatic references, or otherwise. A bid is considered not made in "Good Faith" when an insolvent or irresponsible person, or a person under the age of eighteen makes it. Regardless of the disclosure of his identity, any bid by a consignor or his agent on a lot consigned by him is deemed to be made in "Good Faith".

16. Nominal Bids. The Auctioneer in its sole discretion may reject nominal bids, small opening bids, or very nominal advances. If a lot bearing estimates fails to open for 40–60% of the low estimate, the Auctioneer may pass the item or may place a protective bid on behalf of the consignor.

17. Lots bearing bidding estimates shall open at Auctioneer's discretion (approximately 50% of the low estimate). In the event that no bid meets or exceeds that opening amount, the lot shall pass as unsold.

18. All items are to be purchased per lot as numerically indicated and no lots will be broken. Bids will be accepted in whole dollar amounts only. No "buy" or "unlimited" bids will be accepted. Off-increment bids may be accepted by the Auctioneer at Signature Auctions and Grand Format Auctions. Auctioneer reserves the right to withdraw, prior to the close, any lots from the Auction.

19. Auctioneer reserves the right to rescind the sale in the event of nonpayment, breach of a warranty, disputed ownership, auctioneer's clerical error or omission in exercising bids and reserves, or otherwise.

20. Auctioneer occasionally experiences Internet and/or Server service outages during which Bidders cannot participate or place bids. If such outage occurs, we may at our discretion extend bidding for the auction. This policy applies only to widespread outages and not to isolated problems that occur in various parts of the country from time to time. Auctioneer periodically schedules system downtime for maintenance and other purposes, which may be covered by the Outage Policy. Bidders unable to place their Bids through the Internet are directed to bid through Client Services at 1-800-872-6467.

21. The Auctioneer or its affiliates may consign items to be sold in the Auction, and may bid on those lots or any other lots. Auctioneer or affiliates expressly reserve the right to modify any such bids at any time prior to the hammer based upon data made known to the Auctioneer or its affiliates. The Auctioneer may extend advances, guarantees, or loans to certain consignors, and may extend financing or other credits at varying rates to certain Bidders in the auction.

22. The Auctioneer has the right to sell certain unsold items after the close of the Auction; Such lots shall be considered sold during the Auction and all these Terms and Conditions shall apply to such sales including but not limited to the Buyer's Premium, return rights, and disclaimers.

Payment:

23. All sales are strictly for cash in United States dollars. Cash includes: U.S. currency, bank wire, cashier checks, travelers checks, and bank money orders, all subject to reporting requirements. Checks may be subject to clearing before delivery of the purchases. Credit Card (Visa or Master Card only) and PayPal payments may be accepted up to $10,000 from non-dealers at the sole discretion of the auctioneer, subject to the following limitations: a) sales are only to the cardholder, b) purchases are shipped to the cardholder's registered and verified address, c) Auctioneer may pre-approve the cardholder's credit line, d) a credit card transaction may not be used in conjunction with any other financing or extended terms offered by the Auctioneer, and must transact immediately upon invoice presentation, e) rights of return are governed by these Terms and Conditions, which supersede those conditions promulgated by the card issuer, f) floor Bidders must present their card.

24. Payment is due upon closing of the Auction session, or upon presentment of an invoice. Auctioneer reserves the right to void an invoice if payment in full is not received within 7 days after the close of the Auction.
25. Lots delivered in the States of Texas, California, or other states where the Auction may be held, are subject to all applicable state and local taxes, unless appropriate permits are on file with us. Bidder agrees to pay Auctioneer the actual amount of tax due in the event that sales tax is not properly collected due to: 1) an expired, inaccurate, inappropriate tax certificate or declaration, 2) an incorrect interpretation of the applicable statute, 3) or any other reason. Lots from different Auctions may not be aggregated for sales tax purposes.
26. In the event that a Bidder's payment is dishonored upon presentment(s), Bidder shall pay the maximum statutory processing fee set by applicable state law.
27. If any Auction invoice submitted by Auctioneer is not paid in full when due, the unpaid balance will bear interest at the highest rate permitted by law from the date of invoice until paid. If the Auctioneer refers any invoice to an attorney for collection, the buyer agrees to pay attorney's fees, court costs, and other collection costs incurred by Auctioneer. If Auctioneer assigns collection to its in-house legal staff, such attorney's time expended on the matter shall be compensated at a rate comparable to the hourly rate of independent attorneys.
28. In the event a successful Bidder fails to pay all amounts due, Auctioneer reserves the right to resell the merchandise, and such Bidder agrees to pay for the reasonable costs of resale, including a 10% seller's commission, and also to pay any difference between the resale price and the price of the previously successful bid.
29. Auctioneer reserves the right to require payment in full in good funds before delivery of the merchandise.
30. Auctioneer shall have a lien against the merchandise purchased by the buyer to secure payment of the Auction invoice. Auctioneer is further granted a lien and the right to retain possession of any other property of the buyer then held by the Auctioneer or its affiliates to secure payment of any Auction invoice or any other amounts due the Auctioneer or affiliates from the buyer. With respect to these lien rights, Auctioneer shall have all the rights of a secured creditor under Article 9 of the Texas Uniform Commercial Code, including but not limited to the right of sale. In addition, with respect to payment of the Auction invoice(s), the buyer waives any and all rights of offset he might otherwise have against the Auctioneer and the consignor of the merchandise included on the invoice. If a Bidder owes Auctioneer or its affiliates on any account, Auctioneer and its affiliates shall have the right to offset such unpaid account by any credit balance due Bidder, and it may secure by possessory lien any unpaid amount by any of the Bidder's property in their possession.
31. Title shall not pass to the successful Bidder until all invoices are paid in full. It is the responsibility of the buyer to provide adequate insurance coverage for the items once they have been delivered.

Delivery; Shipping and Handling Charges:

32. Shipping and handling charges will be added to invoices. Please refer to Auctioneer's website www.HA.com/common/shipping.php for the latest charges or call Auctioneer. Auctioneer is unable to combine purchases from other auctions or affiliates into one package for shipping purposes.
33. Successful overseas Bidders shall provide written shipping instructions, including specified customs declarations, to the Auctioneer for any lots to be delivered outside of the United States. NOTE: Declaration value shall be the item(s) hammer price together with its buyer's premium.
34. All shipping charges will be borne by the successful Bidder. Any risk of loss during shipment will be borne by the buyer following Auctioneer's delivery to the designated common carrier or third-party shipper, regardless of domestic or foreign shipment.
35. Due to the nature of some items sold, it shall be the responsibility for the successful bidder to arrange pick-up and shipping through third-parties; as to such items Auctioneer shall have no liability.
36. Any request for shipping verification for undelivered packages must be made within 30 days of shipment by Auctioneer.

Cataloging, Warranties and Disclaimers:

37. NO WARRANTY, WHETHER EXPRESSED OR IMPLIED, IS MADE WITH RESPECT TO ANY DESCRIPTION OR CONDITION REPORT CONTAINED IN THIS AUCTION OR ANY SECOND OPINE. Any description of the items or second opine contained in this Auction is for the sole purpose of identifying the items for those Bidders who do not have the opportunity to view the lots prior to bidding, and no description of items has been made part of the basis of the bargain or has created any express warranty that the goods would conform to any description made by Auctioneer.
38. Auctioneer is selling only such right or title to the items being sold as Auctioneer may have by virtue of consignment agreements on the date of auction and disclaims any warranty of title to the Property. Auctioneer disclaims any warranty of merchantability or fitness for any particular purposes.
39. Translations of foreign language documents may be provided as a convenience to interested parties. Heritage makes no representation as to the accuracy of those translations and will not be held responsible for errors in bidding arising from inaccuracies in translation.
40. Auctioneer disclaims all liability for damages, consequential or otherwise, arising out of or in connection with the sale of any Property by Auctioneer to Bidder. No third party may rely on any benefit of these Terms and Conditions and any rights, if any, established hereunder are personal to the Bidder and may not be assigned. Any statement made by the Auctioneer is an opinion and does not constitute a warranty or representation. No employee of Auctioneer may alter these Terms and Conditions, and, unless signed by a principal of Auctioneer, any such alteration is null and void.
41. Auctioneer shall not be liable for breakage of glass or damage to frames (patent or latent); such defects, in any event, shall not be a basis for any claim for return or reduction in purchase price.

Release:

42. In consideration of participation in the Auction and the placing of a bid, Bidder expressly releases Auctioneer, its officers, directors and employees, its affiliates, and its outside experts that provide second opines, from any and all claims, cause of action, chose of action, whether at law or equity or any arbitration or mediation rights existing under the rules of any professional society or affiliation based upon the assigned description, or a derivative theory, breach of warranty express or implied, representation or other matter set forth within these Terms and Conditions of Auction or otherwise. In the event of a claim, Bidder agrees that such rights and privileges conferred therein are strictly construed as specifically declared herein; e.g., authenticity, typographical error, etc. and are the exclusive remedy. Bidder, by non-compliance to these express terms of a granted remedy, shall waive any claim against Auctioneer.

Dispute Resolution and Arbitration Provision:

43. By placing a bid or otherwise participating in the auction, Bidder accepts these Terms and Conditions of Auction, and specifically agrees to the alternative dispute resolution provided herein. Arbitration replaces the right to go to court, including the right to a jury trial.
44. Auctioneer in no event shall be responsible for consequential damages, incidental damages, compensatory damages, or other damages arising from the auction of any lot. In the event that Auctioneer cannot deliver the lot or subsequently it is established that the lot lacks title, provenance, authenticity, or other transfer or condition issue is claimed, Auctioneer's liability shall be limited to rescission of sale and refund of purchase price; in no case shall Auctioneer's maximum liability exceed the high bid on that lot, which bid shall be deemed for all purposes the value of the lot. After one year has elapsed, Auctioneer's maximum liability shall be limited to any commissions and fees Auctioneer earned on that lot.
45. In the event of an attribution error, Auctioneer may at its sole discretion, correct the error on the Internet, or, if discovered at a later date, to refund the buyer's purchase price without further obligation.
46. If any dispute arises regarding payment, authenticity, grading, description, provenance, or any other matter pertaining to the Auction, the Bidder or a participant in the Auction and/or the Auctioneer agree that the dispute shall be submitted, if otherwise mutually unresolved, to binding arbitration in accordance with the commercial rules of the American Arbitration Association (A.A.A.). A.A.A. arbitration shall be conducted under the provisions of the Federal Arbitration Act with locale in Dallas, Texas. Any claim made by a Bidder has to be presented within one (1) year or it is barred. The prevailing party may be awarded his reasonable attorney's fees and costs. An award granted in arbitration is enforceable in any court of competent jurisdiction. No claims of any kind (except for reasons of authenticity) can be considered after the settlements have been made with the consignors. Any dispute after the settlement date is strictly between the Bidder and consignor without involvement or responsibility of the Auctioneer.
47. In consideration of their participation in or application for the Auction, a person or entity (whether the successful Bidder, a Bidder, a purchaser and/or other Auction participant or registrant) agrees that all disputes in any way relating to, arising under, connected with, or incidental to these Terms and Conditions and purchases, or default in payment thereof, shall be arbitrated pursuant to the arbitration provision. In the event that any matter including actions to compel arbitration, construe the agreement, actions in aid or arbitration or otherwise needs to be litigated, such litigation shall be exclusively in the Courts of the State of Texas, in Dallas County, Texas, and if necessary the corresponding appellate courts. The successful Bidder, purchaser, or Auction participant also expressly submits himself to the personal jurisdiction of the State of Texas.
48. These Terms & Conditions provide specific remedies for occurrences in the auction and delivery process. Where such remedies are afforded, they shall be interpreted strictly. Bidder agrees that any claim shall utilize such remedies; Bidder making a claim in excess of those remedies provided in these Terms and Conditions agrees that in no case whatsoever shall Auctioneer's maximum liability exceed the high bid on that lot, which bid shall be deemed for all purposes the value of the lot..

Miscellaneous:

49. Agreements between Bidders and consignors to effectuate a non-sale of an item at Auction, inhibit bidding on a consigned item to enter into a private sale agreement for said item, or to utilize the Auctioneer's Auction to obtain sales for non-selling consigned items subsequent to the Auction, are strictly prohibited. If a subsequent sale of a previously consigned item occurs in violation of this provision, Auctioneer reserves the right to charge Bidder the applicable Buyer's Premium and consignor a Seller's Commission as determined for each auction venue and by the terms of the seller's agreement.
50. Acceptance of these Terms and Conditions qualifies Bidder as a Heritage customer who has consented to be contacted by Heritage in the future. In conformity with "do-not-call" regulations promulgated by the Federal or State regulatory agencies, participation by the Bidder is affirmative consent to being contacted at the phone number shown in his application and this consent shall remain in effect until it is revoked in writing. Heritage may from time to time contact Bidder concerning sale, purchase, and auction opportunities available through Heritage and its affiliates and subsidiaries.

State Notices:

Notice as to an Auction in California. Auctioneer has in compliance with Title 2.95 of the California Civil Code as amended October 11, 1993 Sec. 1812.600, posted with the California Secretary of State its bonds for it and its employees, and the auction is being conducted in compliance with Sec. 2338 of the Commercial Code and Sec. 535 of the Penal Code.

Notice as to an Auction in New York City. These Terms and Conditions are designed to conform to the applicable sections of the New York City Department of Consumer Affairs Rules and Regulations as Amended. This is a Public Auction Sale conducted by Auctioneer. The New York City licensed Auctioneers are Kathleen Guzman, No.0762165-Day, and Samuel W. Foose, No.0952360-Day, No.0952361-Night, who will conduct the Auction on behalf of Heritage Auctions, Inc. ("Auctioneer"). All lots are subject to: the consignor's right to bid thereon in accord with these Terms and Conditions of Auction, consignor's option to receive advances on their consignments, and Auctioneer, in its sole discretion, may offer limited extended financing to registered bidders, in accord with Auctioneer's internal credit standards. A registered bidder may inquire whether a lot is subject to an advance or reserve. Auctioneer has made advances to various consignors in this sale.

Rev. 10_6_06

ADDITIONAL TERMS AND CONDITIONS OF AUCTION

COINS and CURRENCY TERM A: Signature Auctions are not on approval. No certified material may be returned because of possible differences of opinion with respect to the grade offered by any third-party organization, dealer, or service. No guarantee of grade is offered for uncertified Property sold and subsequently submitted to a third-party grading service. There are absolutely no exceptions to this policy. Under extremely limited circumstances, (e.g. gross cataloging error) a purchaser, who did not bid from the floor, may request Auctioneer to evaluate voiding a sale: such request must be made in writing detailing the alleged gross error; submission of the lot to the Auctioneer must be pre-approved by the Auctioneer; and bidder must notify Ron Brackemyre (1-800-872-6467 ext. 312) in writing of such request within three (3) days of the non-floor bidder's receipt of the lot. Any lot that is to be evaluated must be in our offices within 30 days after Auction. Grading or method of manufacture do not qualify for this evaluation process nor do such complaints constitute a basis to challenge the authenticity of a lot. AFTER THAT 30-DAY PERIOD, NO LOTS MAY BE RETURNED FOR REASONS OTHER THAN AUTHENTICITY. Lots returned must be housed intact in their original holder. No lots purchased by floor Bidders may be returned (including those Bidders acting as agents for others) except for authenticity. Late remittance for purchases may be considered just cause to revoke all return privileges.

COINS and CURRENCY TERM B: Auctions conducted solely on the Internet THREE (3) DAY RETURN POLICY: Certified Coin and Uncertified Currency lots paid for within seven days of the Auction closing are sold with a three (3) day return privilege. Third party graded notes are not returnable for any reason whatsoever. You may return lots under the following conditions: Within three days of receipt of the lot, you must first notify Auctioneer by contacting Client Service by phone (1-800-872-6467) or e-mail (Bid@HA.com), and immediately ship the lot(s) fully insured to the attention of Returns, Heritage, 3500 Maple Avenue, 17th Floor, Dallas TX 75219-3941. Lots must be housed intact in their original holder and condition. You are responsible for the insured, safe delivery of any lots. A non-negotiable return fee of 5% of the purchase price ($10 per lot minimum) will be deducted from the refund for each returned lot or billed directly. Postage and handling fees are not refunded. After the three-day period (from receipt), no items may be returned for any reason. Late remittance for purchases revokes these Return privileges.

COINS and CURRENCY TERM C: Bidders who have inspected the lots prior to any Auction will not be granted any return privileges, except for reasons of authenticity.

COINS and CURRENCY TERM D: Coins sold referencing a third-party grading service are sold "as is" without any express or implied warranty, except for a guarantee by Auctioneer that they are genuine. Certain warranties may be available from the grading services and the Bidder is referred to them for further details: ANACS, P.O. Box 182141, Columbus, Ohio 43218-2141; Numismatic Guaranty Corporation (NGC), P.O. Box 4776, Sarasota, FL 34230; Professional Coin Grading Service (PCGS), PO Box 9458, Newport Beach, CA 92658; and Independent Coin Grading Co. (ICG), 7901 East Belleview Ave., Suite 50, Englewood, CO 80111.

COINS and CURRENCY TERM E: Notes sold referencing a third-party grading service are sold "as is" without any express or implied warranty, except for guarantee by Auctioneer that they are genuine. Grading, condition or other attributes of any lot may have a material effect on its value, and the opinion of others, including third-party grading services such as PCGS Currency, PMG, and CGA may differ with that of Auctioneer. Auctioneer shall not be bound by any prior or subsequent opinion, determination, or certification by any grading service. Bidder specifically waives any claim to right of return of any item because of the opinion, determination, or certification, or lack thereof, by any grading service. Certain warranties may be available from the grading services and the Bidder is referred to them for further details: Paper Money Guaranty (PMG), PO Box 4711, Sarasota FL 34230; PCGS Currency, PO Box 9458, Newport Beach, CA 92658; Currency Grading & Authentication (CGA), PO Box 418, Three Bridges, NJ 08887. Third party graded notes are not returnable for any reason whatsoever.

COINS and CURRENCY TERM F: Since we cannot examine encapsulated coins or notes, they are sold "as is" without our grading opinion, and may not be returned for any reason. Auctioneer shall not be liable for any patent or latent defect or controversy pertaining to or arising from any encapsulated collectible. In any such instance, purchaser's remedy, if any, shall be solely against the service certifying the collectible.

COINS and CURRENCY TERM G: Due to changing grading standards over time, differing interpretations, and to possible mishandling of items by subsequent owners, Auctioneer reserves the right to grade items differently than shown on certificates from any grading service that accompany the items. Auctioneer also reserves the right to grade items differently than the grades shown in the prior catalog should such items be reconsigned to any future auction.

COINS and CURRENCY TERM H: Although consensus grading is employed by most grading services, it should be noted as aforesaid that grading is not an exact science. In fact, it is entirely possible that if a lot is broken out of a plastic holder and resubmitted to another grading service or even to the same service, the lot could come back with a different grade assigned.

COINS and CURRENCY TERM I: Certification does not guarantee protection against the normal risks associated with potentially volatile markets. The degree of liquidity for certified coins and collectibles will vary according to general market conditions and the particular lot involved. For some lots there may be no active market at all at certain points in time.

COINS and CURRENCY TERM J: All non-certified coins and currency are guaranteed genuine, but are not guaranteed as to grade, since grading is a matter of opinion, an art and not a science, and therefore the opinion rendered by the Auctioneer or any third party grading service may not agree with the opinion of others (including trained experts), and the same expert may not grade the same item with the same grade at two different times. Auctioneer has graded the non-certified numismatic items, in the Auctioneer's opinion, to their current interpretation of the American Numismatic Association's standards as of the date the catalog was prepared. There is no guarantee or warranty implied or expressed that the grading standards utilized by the Auctioneer will meet the standards of any grading service at any time in the future.

COINS and CURRENCY TERM K: Storage of purchased coins and currency: Purchasers are advised that certain types of plastic may react with a coin's metal or transfer plasticizer to notes and may cause damage. Caution should be used to avoid storage in materials that are not inert.

COINS and CURRENCY TERM L: NOTE: Purchasers of rare coins or currency through Heritage have available the option of arbitration by the Professional Numismatists Guild (PNG); if an election is not made within ten (10) days of an unresolved dispute, Auctioneer may elect either PNG or A.A.A. Arbitration.

Mail Bidding at Auction

Mail bidding at auction is fun and easy and only requires a few simple steps.

1. Look through the catalog, and determine the lots of interest.

2. Research their market value by checking price lists and other price guidelines.

3. Fill out your bid sheet, entering your maximum bid on each lot using your price research and your desire to own the lot.

4. Verify your bids!

5. Mail Early. Preference is given to the first bids received in case of a tie. When bidding by mail, you frequently purchase items at less than your maximum bid.

Bidding is opened at the published increment above the second highest mail or Internet bid; we act on your behalf as the highest mail bidder. If bidding proceeds, we act as your agent, bidding in increments over the previous bid. This process is continued until you are awarded the lot or you are outbid.

An example of this procedure: You submit a bid of $100, and the second highest mail bid is at $50. Bidding starts at $51 on your behalf. If no other bids are placed, you purchase the lot for $51. If other bids are placed, we bid for you in the posted increments until we reach your maximum bid of $100. If bidding passes your maximum: if you are bidding through the Internet, we will contact you by e-mail; if you bid by mail, we take no other action. Bidding continues until the final bidder wins.

Mail Bidding Instructions

1. **Name, Address, City, State, Zip**
Your address is needed to mail your purchases. We need your telephone number to communicate any problems or changes that may affect your bids.

2. **References**
If you have not established credit with us from previous auctions, you must send a 25% deposit, or list dealers with whom you have credit established.

3. **Lot Numbers and Bids**
List all lots you desire to purchase. On the reverse are additional columns; you may also use another sheet. Under "Amount" enter the maximum you would pay for that lot (whole dollar amounts only). We will purchase the lot(s) for you as much below your bids as possible.

4. **Total Bid Sheet**
Add up all bids and list that total in the appropriate box.

5. **Sign Your Bid Sheet**
By signing the bid sheet, you have agreed to abide by the Terms of Auction listed in the auction catalog.

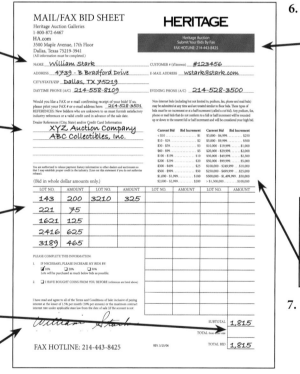

6. **Fax Your Bid Sheet**
When time is short submit a Mail Bid Sheet on our exclusive Fax Hotline. There's no faster method to get your bids to us *instantly*. Simply use the **Heritage Fax Hotline number: 214-443-8425.**

When you send us your original after faxing, mark it "Confirmation of Fax" (preferably in red!)

7. **Bidding Increments**
To facilitate bidding, please consult the following chart. Bids will be accepted on the increments or on the half increments.

The official prices realized list that accompanies our auction catalogs is reserved for bidders and consignors only. We are happy to mail one to others upon receipt of $1.00. Written requests should be directed to Customer Service.

Interactive Internet™ Bidding

You can now bid with Heritage's exclusive *Interactive Internet™* program, available only at our web site: HA.com. It's fun, and it's easy!

1. Register online at: **HA.com**

2. View the full-color photography of every single lot in the online catalog!

3. Construct your own personal catalog for preview.

4. View the current opening bids on lots you want; review the prices realized archive.

5. Bid and receive immediate notification if you are the top bidder; later, if someone else bids higher, you will be notified automatically by e-mail.

6. The *Interactive Internet™* program opens the lot on the floor at one increment over the second highest bid. As the high bidder, your secret maximum bid will compete for you during the floor auction, and it is possible that you may be outbid on the floor after Internet bidding closes. Bid early, as the earliest bird wins in the event of a tie bid.

7. After the sale, you will be notified of your success. It's that easy!

Interactive Internet™ Bidding Instructions

1. **Log Onto Website**

   Log onto **HA.com** and choose the portal you're interested in (i.e., coins, comics, movie posters, fine arts, etc.).

2. **Search for Lots**

   Search or browse for the lot you are interested in. You can do this from the home page, from the Auctions home page, or from the home page for the particular auction in which you wish to participate.

3. **Select Lots**

   Click on the link or the photo icon for the lot you want to bid on.

4. **Enter Bid**

   At the top of the page, next to a small picture of the item, is a box outlining the current bid. Enter the amount of your secret maximum bid in the textbox next to "Secret Maximum Bid." The secret maximum bid is the maximum amount you are willing to pay for the item you are bidding on (for more information about bidding and bid increments, please see the section labeled "Bidding Increments" elsewhere in this catalog). Click on the button marked "Place Absentee Bid." A new area on the same page will open up for you to enter your username (or e-mail address) and password. Enter these, then click "Place Absentee Bid" again.

5. **Confirm Absentee Bid**

   You are taken to a page labeled, "Please Confirm Your Bid." This page shows you the name of the item you're bidding on, the current bid, and the maximum bid. When you are satisfied that all the information shown is correct, click on the button labeled, "Confirm Bid."

6. **Bidding Status Notification**

   One of two pages is now displayed.

   a. If your bid is the current high bid, you will be notified and given additional information as to what might happen to affect your high bidder status over the course of the remainder of the auction. You will also receive a Bid Confirmation notice via email.

   b. If your bid is not the current high bid, you will be notified of that fact and given the opportunity to increase your bid.

CATALOGERS

Mark Van Winkle - Cataloger
Chief Cataloger Mark Van Winkle has worked for Heritage (and previously Steve Ivy) since 1979. He has been Chief Cataloger of Heritage Auction Galleries since 1990, and as such has handled some of the premier numismatic rarities that have been sold at public auction since that time. Mark's literary achievements are considerable also. He was editor of Legacy magazine, won the 1989 NLG award for Best U.S. Commercial Magazine, and the next year won another NLG award for Best Article with his "Interview With John Ford." In 1996 he was awarded the NLG's Best Numismatic Article "Changing Concepts of Liberty," and was accorded a third place Heath Literary Award that same year. He has also done extensive research and published his findings on Branch Mint Proof Morgan Dollars, in addition to writing numerous articles for Coin World and Numismatic News, Mark has also contributed to past editions of the Red Book, and helped with the Standard Silver series in Andrew Pollock's United States Patterns and Related Issues. He was also a contributor to The Guide Book of Double Eagle Gold Coins.

Mark Borckardt - Cataloger
Senior Cataloger Mark Borckardt started attending coin shows and conventions as a dealer in 1970, and has been a full-time professional numismatist since 1980. He received the Early American Coppers Literary Award, and the Numismatic Literary Guild's Book of the Year Award, for the Encyclopedia of Early United States Cents, 1793-1814, published in 2000. He serves as a contributor to A Guide Book of United States Coins, and has contributed to many references, including the Harry W. Bass, Jr. Sylloge, and the Encyclopedia of Silver Dollars and Trade Dollars of the United States. Most recently, he was Senior Numismatist with Bowers and Merena Galleries, serving as a major contributor to all of that firm's landmark auctions, as well as the Rare Coin Review. Mark is a life member of the American Numismatic Association, and an active member of numerous numismatic organizations. He is an avid collector of numismatic literature, holding several thousand volumes in his library, as well as numismatic related postcards and ephemera. When not immersed in numismatics, he is an avid bowler, carrying an average just over 200, and with seven perfect 300 games. Mark is a graduate of the University of Findlay (Ohio) with a Bachelors Degree in Mathematics. Mark and his wife have a 20-something year old son, and twin daughters who are enrolled at Baylor.

Brian Koller - Cataloger
Catalog Production Manager Brian Koller's attention to detail ensures that every catalog, printed and on-line, is as error free as technology and human activity allows. In addition to his coin cataloging duties, he also helps with consignor promises and customer service issues. Brian has been a Heritage Auctions cataloger since 2001, and before that he worked as a telecom software engineer for 16 years. He is a graduate of Iowa State University with a Bachelor's degree in Computer Engineering, and is an avid collector of U.S. gold coins. Brian's numismatic footnote is as discoverer of a 1944-D half dollar variety that has the designer's monogram engraved by hand onto a working die. In addition to describing many thousands of coins in Heritage catalogs, Brian has written more than one thousand reviews of classic movies, which can be found on his website, filmsgraded.com.

John Salyer - Cataloger
Cataloger John Salyer has been a numismatist and coin cataloger with Heritage since October of 2002. John began collecting Lincoln Cents, Jefferson Nickels, Mercury and Roosevelt Dimes, and Franklin Halves at the age of eleven, as a sixth-grader in Fort Worth; his best friend was also a collector, and his dad would drive them to coin shops and flea markets in search of numismatic treasures. The two youngsters even mowed lawns together in order to purchase their coins, which were always transferred into Whitman folders. John graduated from the University of Texas with a bachelor's degree in English. Prior to his numismatic employment, he worked primarily within the federal government and for several major airlines. His hobbies include playing guitar and collecting antique postcards; as an avid golfer, he also enjoys spending time on the links. John has enjoyed making his former hobby his current occupation, and he still actively collects coins.

Jon Amato - Cataloger
Cataloger Jon Amato has been with Heritage since March 2004. He was previously a Program Manager in the New York State Department of Economic Development, and an Adjunct Professor at the State University of New York at Albany, where he taught economic geography, natural disasters assessment, and environmental management. Jon is currently writing a monograph on the numismatic history and rarity of the draped bust, small eagle half dollars of 1796-1797. His research included surveying more than 4,000 auction catalogs, recording the descriptions, grades, and photos of 1796-1797 halves. He published an article entitled "Surviving 1796-1797 Draped Bust Half Dollars and their Grade Distribution," in the John Reich Journal, February 2005, Vol. 16, Issue 2, and also wrote "An Analysis of 1796-1797 Draped Bust Half Dollars," in The Numismatist, Sept. 2001, Vol. 114, No. 9. Jon belongs to many numismatic organizations, including the ANA, ANS, John Reich Collectors Society, and the Liberty Seated Collectors Club, and has made several presentations at ANA Numismatic Theaters. He earned a bachelor's degree from Arizona State University, an M.A. from the State University of New York at Buffalo, and a Ph. D. from the University of Toronto.

Greg Lauderdale - Cataloger
Cataloger Greg Lauderdale grew up in Dallas, and he began working in a coin shop there in 1979. His interest in numismatics and his trading skills blossomed, and he became a Life Member of the ANA only two years later in 1981. During the 1980s, he conducted several coin auctions in the Dallas Area, including several for the Dallas Coin Club show. He first contracted with Heritage Auction Galleries to help write the 1985 Baltimore ANA auction catalog. He joined Heritage full-time in September of 1985, working as a cataloger and a coin buyer. Greg "left" Heritage in 1988 to develop his personal rare coin company, but has continued to split his time between cataloging for Heritage and trading on eBay from his new home in Maui. In addition to his numismatic sales, Greg has developed into quite a 'presence' in the world of rare and early Hawaiian postcards. For those bidders who attend Heritage's auctions in person, Greg can often be seen working at the front table – one of the few catalogers in America who is actively involved in the selling process!

John Beety - Cataloger
Cataloger John Dale Beety grew up in Logansport, Indiana, a small town associated with several numismatic luminaries. Highlights as a Young Numismatist include attending Pittman III, four ANA Summer Seminars (thanks to various YN scholarships), and placing third in the 2001 World Series of Numismatics with Eric Li Cheung. He accepted a position with Heritage as a cataloger immediately after graduation from Rose-Hulman Institute of Technology after serving an internship at Heritage during the summer of 2004. In addition to his numismatic interests, he enjoys many types of games, with two state junior titles in chess and an appearance in the Top 20 Juniors list of the World Blitz Chess Association.

INDIAN HALF EAGLES

Beautifully Toned MS66 1908 Five Dollar

3150   1908 MS66 PCGS. First year of the new Pratt design and widely saved, presumably because of the novelty of the design as well as the radical departure from the long-lived Coronet type. The reduced relief used by Pratt on the quarter eagle and half eagle coins that began production in 1908, made the field the highpoint of the coin. As a result, the rim that formerly protected the interior designs of the coronet coinage were no longer present and the fields were susceptible to abrading from even the slightest contact. Thus, the difficulty in locating this design in Gem and better condition. This particular coin shows no obvious marks on either side and sharp striking definition. The surfaces are bright and lustrous with a lovely mixture of rose-gold and lilac color on each side. Population: 16 in 66, 1 finer (11/06).
From The Kutasi Collection.(#8510)

Pleasing Gem 1908-S Half Eagle

3151   1908-S MS65 PCGS. The useful Garrett-Guth *Gold Encyclopedia* (2006) comments regarding this issue, "If a single coin is desired from this series, this date and mint should be considered for the overall quality and availability." This Gem piece does not disappoint in that respect, offering problem-free surfaces with deep, mellow orange-gold color, essentially no abrasions, and excellent overall eye appeal. The strike is also fairly well executed, save for light softness near the lower obverse border. Population: 37 in 65, 20 finer (11/06).
From The Kutasi Collection.(#8512)

Lustrous Near-Gem 1909-S Half Eagle Rarity

3152   1909-S MS64 PCGS. This is a sharply struck example, as are most, and it exhibits beautiful deep orange-gold color with frosty luster. David Akers has estimated that fewer than 20 pieces exist in MS64 or better grades, and current population data seems to support his words, written 20 years ago: "The 1909-S is one of the four or five rarest issues of the series. Among San Francisco Mint issues it is virtually on a par with the 1915-S and is far more rare than the lower mintages 1908-S. Mint State examples at any level are rare and in the high Mint State grades, i.e. MS-64 or better, there are probably fewer than 20 specimens in all." Population: 16 in 64, 4 finer (11/06).
From The Kutasi Collection.(#8516)

Pleasing Gem 1910 Indian Five

3153   1910 MS65 PCGS. This pleasing Gem of a fairly available issue, like most of the emission, is quite appealing and well produced. A light sunset-orange tinge greets the viewer, with distraction-free, appealing surfaces that complement a bold strike and excellent eye appeal. The Indian's cheek is essentially free of visible contact. Gems of this issue are available for a price, making this a good selection for a high grade gold type set. This piece is one of 17 so certified at PCGS, with none finer (11/06). Certified in a green-label holder.
From The Kutasi Collection.(#8517)

Attractive, Colorful MS65 1912 Five Dollar

3154   1912 MS65 PCGS. Because of the conditional scarcity of Indian half eagles and the subsequent high prices these pieces command when offered at public auction, most collectors have rethought their collecting strategy and included MS64 coins rather than the Gems that might be sought in other series. The 1912 is one of the few issues of this type that is relatively available as a Gem. It is therefore a coin that can be used for type purposes as well. According to the November population data from both PCGS and NGC, a total of 74 coins have been certified in MS65, but only three are finer (all NGC). The fragile surfaces of this piece are barely abraded, and each side displays generous amounts of rose-gold and lilac patina with strong underlying mint frost. A well struck example of this so-called "common" date in the five dollar Indian series.
From The Kutasi Collection.(#8523)

Near-Gem 1914-S Five Dollar, A Major Condition Rarity Among 20th Century Gold

3155   1914-S MS64 PCGS. The 1914-S five dollar is one of those issues that may not "ring a bell" with most collectors. It is an unusual issue that is rarely encountered in MS64 condition. Much of the reason for this scarcity in high grade has to do with the method of manufacture of these pieces. To quote Akers (1988): " ... the surfaces are nearly always granular and decidedly lacklustre." So, by definition the 1914-S is not a coin that one can expect to locate in high grades. That is borne out by the number (or rather lack thereof) of MS64 and MS65 pieces that have been certified. Only 11 coins have been graded in MS64 (seven at PCGS and four at NGC), and there is only one Gem (an NGC coin). The reason for the high grade of this piece has to do with the next sentence in Akers' 1988 book: "A very few specimens, however, have a somewhat satiny look and excellent lustre that compares favorably to a nice 1910-S, for example." This is such a coin and it exhibits bright, satiny luster. It also shows rich reddish-gold color with lilac patina interspersed over both sides. The striking definition is also strongly brought up on both obverse and reverse, and of course, there are no noticeable or detracting blemishes aside from the usual, small abrasions seen in the fields of this design type.

This is highest graded '14-S we have offered for sale since the 2004 ANA sale when we sold the lone MS65 for $63,250. The 1914-S is one of the great condition rarities in 20th century U.S. gold. This coin represents one of the few opportunities the specialist will have to purchase a piece that has both technical merit as well as the elusive eye appeal that is almost never found on a '14-S.

From The Kutasi Collection.(#8529)

MS64 1915-S Five, One of the Finest at PCGS

3156   1915-S MS64 PCGS. The mintage of San Francisco Mint half eagles in 1915 plummeted almost 40% from the year-ago levels, to 164,000 pieces, and this issue is among the most elusive of the series in all grades, and even more so in Mint State. PCGS and NGC have each graded only nine pieces in MS64, with a single piece at NGC reaching the MS65 level (11/06). This satiny, lustrous piece offers two-toned, gorgeous surfaces with generous dollops of sunset-orange complementing tinges of hazel on the highpoints of each side. The strike is fairly well executed, with softness mostly limited to a few of the lower headdress feathers, and the reverse appears high-end for the grade. A nice piece, and aesthetically unlikely to be surpassed. Population: 9 in 64, 0 finer (11/06).
From The Kutasi Collection.(#8531)

Gem Mint State 1916-S Half Eagle

3157   1916-S MS65 PCGS. Advanced collectors of Indian Head half eagles seldom have an opportunity to acquire such a fine quality example of this date as only a few Gem pieces are known. This specimen has rich orange and rose colored gold surfaces with frosty luster. It is well struck with sharp obverse and reverse details throughout. A rather large hoard of these coins was discovered a number of years ago, but nearly all pieces from that hoard were at the lowest Mint State grade levels. This example, apparently not from the hoard, is an aesthetically superior Gem. Population: 8 in 65, 3 finer (11/06).
From The Kutasi Collection.(#8532)

Choice Mint State 1929 Half Eagle

3158   1929 MS64 PCGS. As rare and well-known as this date is to collectors, it is only ranked as the ninth rarest date according to Akers. This is because the entire mintage was saved from circulation, and eventually stored in vaults. Most were later melted, although some examples were saved from the melting pot and entered numismatic circulation. This example is a sharply struck specimen with frosty yellow-gold luster and excellent visual appeal. It is also a remarkable piece for its quality and it barely misses finest known honors. Population: 96 in 64, 8 finer (11/06).
From The Kutasi Collection.(#8533)

INDIAN EAGLES

Exceptionally Well Preserved
Wire Rim 1907 Ten, MS66 PCGS

3159   1907 Wire Rim MS66 PCGS. In 1907 the first coin struck of the Saint-Gaudens designs was the ten dollar gold piece. This featured a portrait of Liberty, wearing an Indian ceremonial headdress on the obverse. The reverse included a standing eagle, facing left, clutching a bundle of arrows with an entwined olive branch. This was derived from the 1905 special inaugural medal by Saint-Gaudens and Weinman.

Ten dollar gold coins of the initial Saint-Gaudens design were prepared from models that had the field curving upward directly to the rim of the coin. This produced a pronounced knife rim (traditionally called a "wire rim") rather than the normal flat rim of circulating coins. This prevented easy stacking of the coins, and they were never intended for general circulation and never distributed to sub-Treasuries or commercial banks. The reverse design had triangular text stops (called "periods" by most) at the ends of each line of inscription. The edge had 46 small stars placed evenly around the circumference. (Note: true patterns had either a plain edge, or 46 irregularly sized and spaced stars.)

Five hundred of the knife rim/periods eagles were struck on a medal press during the last days of August and the first part of September 1907. The work was done so that if President Roosevelt called for some of the Saint-Gaudens design coins, the mint would be able to provide them. The eagles, along with the High Relief double eagles, were distributed at face value to Cabinet members, Congressmen, Federal judges, Treasury officials, and others who requested them, including private citizens and museums. In late December an additional 42 pieces were struck, making a total mintage of 542 pieces.

Eagles that remained undistributed by mid-December were shipped to the Treasury Department in Washington, D.C., and remained there for several years. In 1912, the Treasurer's coins were counted and found to contain 129 of the knife rim/periods ten dollar gold pieces. Over the next year, 59 pieces were sold to coin dealers Tom Elder and Henry Chapman, with a few to Treasury employees, for $15 each. The proceeds went into the Philadelphia Mint Collection fund. Seventy pieces could not be sold at a premium and were melted. Thus, the maximum quantity available to coin collectors is 472 pieces. Examples that are noticeably worn were probably kept as pocket pieces. Many examples were handled roughly over the past century and have numerous dings and abrasions. Quite a few specimens have a partial fin due to a mismatch between face and edge dies. The fin (also called a "Wire Rim") was considered by the mint as a defect and does not indicate the coin was struck with abnormally high pressure.

As with all Wire Rim tens, this piece shows pronounced die polishing marks in the fields and bright, satiny mint luster. However, rather than the usual bright yellow-gold color normally seen on these pieces, this coin has taken on a light overlay of reddish patina with the passage of time. Virtually perfect surfaces; there are no obvious or distracting contact marks on either side of this magnificent coin.
From The Kutasi Collection.(#8850)

1907 ROLLED RIM EAGLE, MS67 PCGS

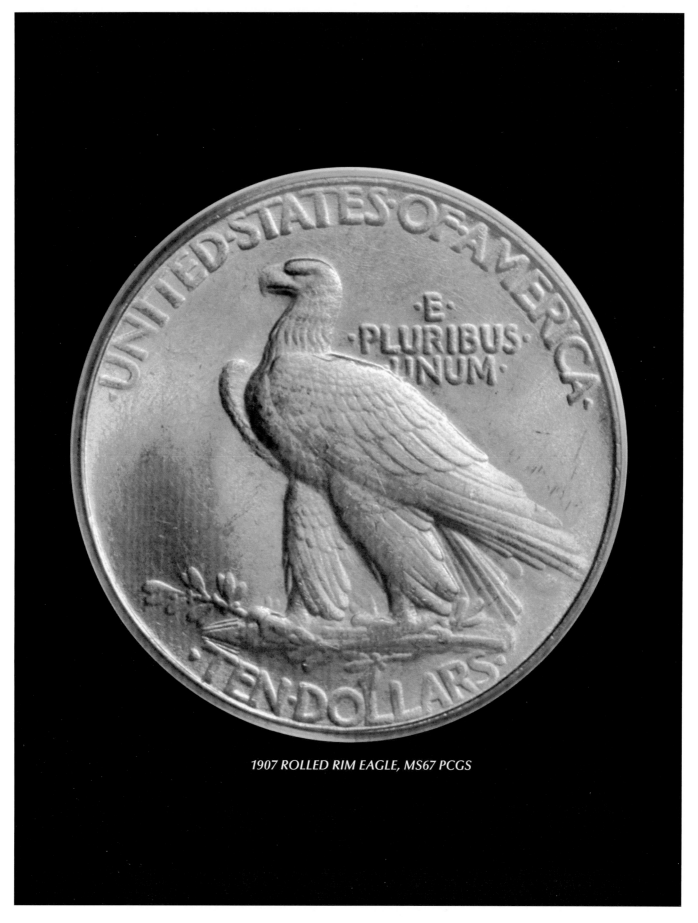

1907 ROLLED RIM EAGLE, MS67 PCGS

One of the Finest Known 1907 Rolled Rim Tens, A Spectacular MS67 PCGS Coin

3160   1907 Rolled Rim MS67 PCGS. This was the second version of the Saint-Gaudens ten dollar design produced in 1907. After plain-edge patterns of the knife rim/periods eagle were struck, Philadelphia Mint Engraver, Charles Barber, realized the lack of a normal rim prevented coins from stacking properly. Believing that these designs might be used for circulation purposes later in the year (not just to satisfy President Roosevelt), Barber used the same models as for the knife rim coins to make new hubs. However, on these new hubs the engraver cut a normal rim so that the pieces would stack. Experimental examples with irregular edge stars were made and the change was approved. But, before production dies could be made, another angry letter arrived from President Roosevelt demanding that coins be struck "by September first" from the first dies. Mint Director George Roberts had resigned in July, and Acting Director Robert Preston ordered 500 of the first variety struck.

Barber's second version with normal rim and periods was then planned for use in striking circulation pieces. Just before large scale production began, a pair of new models arrived from Saint-Gaudens' estate. According to Barber, these models were satisfactory for circulation use and he recommended they be used in place of his rim-added version. Acting Director Preston apparently became confused about the different versions of the ten dollar coin, and ordered production use of Barber's version, over the objections of Barber and other Philadelphia Mint officials. Thirty-one thousand five hundred pieces were struck in late September and seemed destined for release to banks across the country. Philadelphia Mint Superintendent John Landis thought the results were inferior and that the mint should issue only pieces made from the new models. As an aside, numismatists today clearly disagree with Superintendent Landis as the Rolled Rim ten is listed as # 52 in the Garrett-Guth reference *100 Greatest U.S. Coins*. He wrote to Acting Director Preston on September 25, 1907, enclosing two examples of the new 1907 eagle design: one the normal rim/periods version, the other a sample made from the new models from Saint-Gaudens' estate. (These later became the normal circulation coins for 1907.)

"You will notice that the eagle from the last model [from Saint-Gaudens' estate—no periods] is a great improvement over those of the first model [the normal rim/with periods]. The latter are indefinite in detail and outline, not being at all sharp and look like imperfect coins or coins that have been sweated, while the former is sharp in outline, the detail shows up well, the border is broad and prominent and the coins will stack perfectly. ...If this last model meets with your approval, I would strongly urge upon you the expediency of immediately replacing the $315,000 now on hand, of the first model with eagles of the last models ... I think we will be severely criticized, and certainly deserve to be, if the eagles already struck should be allowed to go into circulation."

Assistant Treasury Secretary John Edwards thought the coins were satisfactory and should be released due to the high demand for gold in commerce. (This was near the beginning of the brief, but serious, 1907 Knickerbocker Panic and public demand for gold coin was high along the East Coast). On November 1, Frank Leach, the new Mint Director, finally assumed full control of his office. One of the first things he did was to countermand the Assistant Secretary's order. Having just come from several years as Superintendent of the San Francisco Mint, Leach's experience told him that Landis was right and the coins were not up to standard for sharpness and overall quality. Leach had all of the 31,500 normal rim/periods coins melted except for 50 pieces kept for distribution to museums and public coin collections. A list of purchasers shows the original owners of many of these coins. Some ended up in the hands of museums or famous collectors such as John Work Garrett, William H. Woodin, and Justice Oliver Wendell Holmes. Others found their way to hobbyists now unknown to collectors. The last recorded sale from the mint was on October 19, 1908 to Dr. S. E. Young of Baywood, Virginia. All of these pieces have normal edge stars. All were struck on normal production presses—not a medal press. The master hubs were destroyed in 1910. While it is universally believed that 40 to 45 pieces have survived today, even great rarities like a Rolled Rim ten Indian can be lost or damaged under extraordinary circumstances. Such is the fate of one MS66 specimen that was stolen by a postal carrier last year. That individual was recently convicted and sentenced to three years in prison for his crime. The coin, however, has vanished and it may be years before it surfaces again, if indeed it ever does.

This piece has lovely, thick mint frost over each side. The fields show a few small swirling die polishing marks, like the Wire Rim tens only to a lesser degree. The surfaces are original with reddish-gold and lilac coloration over both obverse and reverse. This is one of the finest Rolled Rim tens known. The two major services have only certified four other pieces in MS67 (two at PCGS and two at NGC), and none are finer (10/06).

From The Kutasi Collection.(#8851)

Superb 1907 No Motto Ten Dollar— One of the Finest Examples Known

3161   1907 No Motto MS67 PCGS. This last version of the 1907 gold eagle is the one used for production of coins that actually made it into circulation. Dies were prepared from a new set of models provided by the Saint-Gaudens' estate and approved by Philadelphia Mint engraver Barber. Overall, the design resulted in sharper looking coins. These were used only through the end of the calendar year 1907. For 1908, a slightly revised version was issued that corrected some of the problems encountered with the 1907 edition.

Only days after approval had been given to use Barber's version with the rim added, a new pair of models arrived from the Saint-Gaudens estate. These had been prepared by Henry Hering and Homer Saint-Gaudens (the sculptor's son) in the lowest relief they believed the artist would have accepted. In addition to a more coinlike relief, the design had more deeply cut details than previous ones and omitted the triangular text stops on the reverse. (By the time the mint made reductions from the models, the triangles had turned into irregular ovals somewhat like periods, or the pellets on medieval coinage.)

Barber immediately pronounced the new models acceptable for coinage and approved them, commenting that production could begin in about a month. When instructions came from Acting Director Preston to strike coins for circulation, the order stipulated they be made from the second models. To Barber, these were the ones just received. But to Preston they were the ones to which Barber had added a rim—really from the first models. The situation was confusing for the 74-year-old Preston, and having the White House and Treasury Secretary breathing down his neck didn't improve the difficult circumstances.

It fell to Frank Leach, who took office as Mint Director on November 1, to resolve the situation. He had all but 50 of the coins struck on Preston's orders melted. He then ordered production of the final variety of ten dollar gold coin from the last models as approved by Barber. The new coins were a significant improvement over the previous versions in detail and mechanical characteristics. Relief was within coinable limits and the rim was wide enough to protect the design. As on the other two versions for 1907, 46 small stars circle the edge of the coin. Over the next decade small changes were made to the design of the eagle to strengthen the feathers, stars, and other parts of the design. Two stars were added to the edge in 1912.

These eagles were the first of the Saint-Gaudens coins to be released into circulation in early November 1907. Their release came several days before the official acceptance of Oklahoma—the forty-sixth state—into the Union, making the starred edge a technical anomaly. But few paid attention to the coin's edge; their attention was drawn to the absence of the religious motto IN GOD WE TRUST from the coin. Within days, letters and petitions of protest were on their way to Congress and the President. Less than a year later the design was modified to include the motto on the reverse. No proofs were issued for coin collectors; however, at least two sandblast proofs with an unusually wide rim are known. We know nothing about when or why they were made.

This is a stunning Superb Gem Mint State example of this date, and one of the very finest graded by either service. Only two pieces have been certified finer—one at PCGS and one at NGC. This production variant of the 1907 ten dollar is known for being well-produced and many are also well-preserved, making it an excellent type coin. The luster on this piece is frosted and bright. Each side shows slight reddish-gold color with occasional lilac accents within the recesses of the design elements. A lovely, pristine example of this important coin—the first of the Saint-Gaudens coinage released into circulation.

From The Kutasi Collection.(#8852)

Original Superb Gem 1908 No Motto Ten Tied for Second Finest Certified

3162   1908 No Motto MS67 PCGS. During December 1907, new hubs and working dies were made for the 1908 eagles. As was normal procedure for the mint's engraving department, Barber and Morgan retouched the master hub and die to better define the stars, date, and inscriptions. Gradual modifications continued for several years into the future. Although the mint was fully aware of Congressional agitation for restoration of the motto IN GOD WE TRUST to the eagles and double eagles, and had already prepared drawings for a half eagle (never issued), work had to concentrate on the No Motto version. The mint also had to make eagle and double eagle dies and edge collars for the Denver and San Francisco Mints. Additionally, they supplied the other mints with a sample of the mechanical attachment that controlled collar segments during striking. As the "mother mint," the Philadelphia staff had to prepare and test everything before sending materials to the other mints. With new designs and mechanical changes, this took much more time than in prior years and meant that branch mints had to wait a month or more before they could begin adapting equipment to their presses. All of this took its toll on the Philadelphia Mint's ability to produce gold eagles as well as other required coins. The result was that only 33,500 No Motto eagles were approved for release by the coiner and superintendent.

Because of the slight hub and die modifications before the 1908 coins were struck, the definition is superior on this date to those seen from 1907. The mint frost on this piece is superior and, like the three 1907 tens from the Kutasi Collection, shows rich rose-gold coloration with lilac accents in the recesses of the design. The fields have a fine granularity, as seen on all tens through 1916. One of only three coins so graded by PCGS with five certified MS67 by NGC, and only one finer (an NGC coin). The most recent sale of this date in Gem condition was the sale of a MS66 example in our April 2006 Central States Signature Sale that realized $51,750.
From The Kutasi Collection.(#8853)

Bright, Frosted MS66
1908-D No Motto Ten Dollar

3163   1908-D No Motto MS66 PCGS. At the beginning of 1908 Frank Downer, Superintendent of the Denver Mint, faced the problem of producing new starred-edge eagles. In late January, he had been sent face dies, edge collars, and a sample mechanism for controlling the collar segments during striking. The Philadelphia Mint mechanics also sent drawings of how they thought the apparatus could be adapted to Denver's presses. Yet, it was up to Downer's staff to make it work.

Initial results were inconsistent, with most of the coins too thick and many errors. The Philadelphia Mint sent out obverse dies made from a new hub and that helped considerably. As the Denver coining department staff gained experience, they successfully adapted the dies and edge collar device to their presses. Within a month production seemed to be moving along smoothly. Overall, use of a segmented edge collar to impart 46 (later 48) small stars on the coin's edge seems to have been easier to manage on the ten dollar coins than the twenties. With 210,000 pieces released for circulation of the 1908-D No Motto, along with a substantial double eagle production, it appears the Denver Mint had successfully adapted its presses to the new design.

In top grades, the 1908-D No Motto is scarce with few examples certified above MS63. Akers (1988) states that this is "one of the least attractive [issues], due largely to the fact that it is generally flatly struck on the obverse and is decidedly lacklustre." However, he goes on to state that there are a small number of exceptions, notably the Kruthoffer coin, that have frosted surfaces and are of superb quality. This piece is definitely one of the exceptions. The surfaces are bright and frosted with an accent of orange-gold color around the margin on the reverse. Strong granularity is also present over each side, as always. Surprisingly sharp for the issue with no obvious or mentionable abrasions. One of only 10 pieces so graded by both of the major services in MS66. A mere three pieces have been certified finer (all by NGC). The most recent sale of this date in MS66 was at the Heritage Central States Signature sale in April 2006, where that coin realized $86,250.
From The Kutasi Collection.(#8854)

Splendid, Richly Patinated MS66
1908 Motto Ten Dollar

3164   1908 Motto MS66 PCGS. Introduction of the new ten dollar gold coin in 1907 was greeted with public objection because of the absence of the customary religious motto. One newspaper reported that Director Leach was expecting complaints as soon as church organizations had time to meet and formulate resolutions of protest. Many complaints were received and by the end of December the mint was planning to add the motto as soon as Congress acted. The Mint Act of 1908 was signed on May 17 and required the addition of "In God We Trust" to all gold coins. The mint had anticipated the law and prepared samples of motto placement in February. These were struck onto small squares of thick paperboard and submitted for approval. Sample coins were struck on May 23 and final approval was given immediately to place the motto on the reverse, in front of the eagle. Beginning with the legislation's effective date of June 17, all the new eagles carried the motto through the end of the series in 1933.

The motto was placed on the reverse, in the blank field in front of the eagle's breast. After producing a modest quantity of No Motto eagles earlier in the year, the Philadelphia Mint accelerated production for the With Motto variety and struck 341,370 pieces for circulation. This superior example shows deep, even orange-gold coloration with fine, matte-like surfaces. Both the obverse and reverse displays bright mint luster and sharp striking details. Conservatively graded at the MS66 grade level, there are no abrasions worthy of mention.

Ex: ANA Platinum Night (Heritage, 7/05), lot 10387, where it realized a still-record price for an MS66 of this issue of $35,650.

From The Kutasi Collection.(#8859)

Finely Granular MS66 PCGS
1908-D Motto Ten Dollar

3165   1908-D Motto MS66 PCGS. Among the factors that resulted in somewhat weakly struck With Motto Denver Mint eagles of 1908 were the difficulties associated with adapting the new obverse, reverse, and edge dies to the mint's equipment. This is consistent with the earlier No Motto pieces. However, once adaptations were made a number of high quality tens were produced with the motto on the reverse. The No Motto tens from Denver are known for pronounced granularity over each side. This tendency was lessened with the Motto coins. This piece is typical with fine-grain surfaces and intense, satiny mint luster—one might even be tempted to call this coin frosted. Each side displays an almost even mixture of rose-gold and lilac coloration, and there are no mentionable abrasions present. The striking details are strong throughout, an indication that this piece may have been a later striking that was produced after the branch mint learned how to use the new dies and edge equipment. This is one of only four pieces that have been so graded by PCGS with an equal number certified by NGC, and seven coins are finer (10/06).

From The Kutasi Collection.(#8860)

Lustrous, Reddish-Tinged MS67 1908-S Ten Dollar

3166   1908-S MS67 PCGS. It was August before Edward Sweeney, Superintendent of the San Francisco Mint, reported, " ... a small run was made on eagles with the new design dies ... they stacked 0.025-inches higher than standard ... the dies were returned to Philadelphia and new dies furnished." The new dies were tested and they also produced coins that were too thick. Sweeney decided that with use the dies would wear slightly and eventually the coins would be within mint guidelines.

Engraver Charles Barber had also been busy stacking eagles and discovered that " ... the pieces are thinner on one part of the coin than on the other ... therefore the pile never measures twice the same." As Barber continued, he shifted responsibility for the coinage problems to Saint-Gaudens. "The many difficulties that we have had to contend with and the very unsatisfactory appearance of the coin ... should convince anyone that although a sculptor may have a reputation in his own line, he is a failure when taken out of it."

Only 59,850 eagles were released by the San Francisco Mint in 1908. All were from new dies that included the motto on the reverse, and the overall quality of these pieces is quite high. While the overall preservation of this coin is far above average, in many ways it also typifies the 1908-S ten. That is, most examples show exceptional mint luster and are either frosted and finely granular or satiny and radiant, as pointed out by Akers (1988). This coin is a frosted variant with the expected fine granularity on each side. Sharply struck throughout, the surfaces are nearly defect-free, and they show a pronounced reddish patina with only a slight hint of lilac present (visible with magnification). While the low mintage is one of the main drawing cards for this issue, specialists know the 1908-S is one of the best, if not *the* best produced of all ten Indians, and a coin of incomparable beauty in high grade. Only seven other pieces have been so graded by PCGS with three in MS67 by NGC, and seven finer at both services combined (10/06). *From The Kutasi Collection.*(#8861)

Richly Patinated and Highly Lustrous MS66 1909 Ten Dollar

3167   1909 MS66 PCGS. For 1909 only eight obverse and nine reverse dies were used to strike 217,235 ten dollar gold pieces. As Roger Burdette points out, "Of the coins made at the Philadelphia Mint, a whopping 32,446—nearly 18%—of the eagles struck were defective in weight or striking. This must have kept the roomful of lady adjustors busy, individually weighing and inspecting each gold coin as they came from the coining room." The net mintage for 1909 was a modest 184,789 pieces, but the overall quality of the issue was quite high. This piece shows the usual satiny finish and it also displays the rich rose and lilac patina that is common to most of the coins from the Kutasi Collection, and yet so uncommon on gold coins in general. Sharply defined throughout with finely granular surfaces, the coin is virtually defect-free. An outstanding example of this rarity in the ten dollar Indian series—only 11 other pieces have been so graded by both PCGS and NGC and a mere five coins are finer (10/06).

From The Kutasi Collection.(#8862)

Upper Condition Census
1909-D Ten Dollar, MS66 PCGS

3168   1909-D MS66 PCGS. The coinage presses in use at the Denver Mint were similar to those at Philadelphia, and the initial adaptation of the segmented, starred edge collar mechanism in 1908 was accomplished in about a month. For 1909 only 121,540 eagles were struck for circulation by the Denver Mint. While this is a low mintage, it is not all that impressive by itself as other issues have an even lower mintage and greater availability in the better grades of Mint State (for instance the 1908-S and 1911-S). What matters the most is the attrition rate, and in the case of the 1909-D ten dollar that rate was very high. In his catalog of the Thaine Price Collection (1998) David Akers states that a number of previously unknown 1909-D tens have come onto the market in recent years. He goes on to say that most of these are of minimal Uncirculated quality, with only a few reaching the Choice level. This statement appears to be an accurate assessment of the current state of the 1909-D ten. The highest grade level that is moderately available is MS64, and the two major grading services combined have only certified 46 pieces in that grade. The dropoff is precipitous above that level with six Gems, eight MS66 coins, and three pieces in MS67 certified (with a certain but unknown number of resubmissions undoubtedly contained in these numbers).

In addition to being one of the absolute rarities in the ten dollar Indian series, the 1909-D is also one of the most consistently attractive. Each side shows even, granular surfaces, much like the previous year's D-mint No Motto issue. However, this is a far better-produced issue that has an overlay of rich, satiny mint luster and a strong strike. Additionally, there are virtually no abrasions present save for an identifying vertical mark on the lower rows of feathers on the eagle's wing. The surfaces have a pronounced reddish patina with lilac surrounding the devices—an unquestionable sign of originality.
From The Kutasi Collection.(#8863)

Exceptionally Lustrous MS67
1909-S Ten Dollar

3169   1909-S MS67 PCGS. Work on the new design San Francisco eagles did not begin until August when a small quantity were struck during the visit of Director Leach. These were found to be too thick and it was not until mid-September that satisfactory coins were struck. Seven obverse and seven reverse dies were used to produce the San Francisco Mint's 1909 eagles. Each die pair struck on average 41,898 coins with total production of 293,287 pieces for the year. The net mintage—coins that were of proper weight, fineness, and without production defects—was 292,350 coins, indicating that just 937 defective pieces were made. Compared to the Philadelphia Mint's defect rate of nearly 3%, it seems the San Francisco Mint staff knew better how to mint these gold coins.

This is certainly a well-produced example of this median rarity in the ten dollar Indian series. The surfaces shout with luster—the bright, swirling cartwheel luster that S-mint coins are so well known for. Akers (1988) classes the 1909-S in two categories: " ... either very frosty with very little granularity, or slightly satiny." This piece is clearly an example of the former finish. Additionally, the striking details are boldly defined throughout, and there are no mentionable marks on either side. The only recorded hoard of this issue was a group of 70-90 pieces found in South America in 1977. Most of these pieces were of MS60-63 quality, which would lead one to the conclusion that this piece is probably not from that hoard and has been in a high grade date or type set since the year of issue. This piece is tied with one other at the MS67 level, and is exceeded only by a single MS68 coin at NGC (10/06). This is the first offering by Heritage of a MS67 example of this date. *From The Kutasi Collection.*(#8864)

Reddish Tinged MS66 1910 Ten Dollar

3170   1910 MS66 PCGS. The 1910 is one of the more available P-mint tens in the ten Indian series. The mintage was a substantial 318,500 pieces and numerous Uncirculated examples were set aside. This issue is available in grades up to and including MS67 (although in very small numbers), and the finest coins known are graded MS68. There are three occurrences of the 1910 in this ultimate grade, but one has to suspect at least one of these grading occurrences is a resubmission. As with all the coins in the Kutasi Collection, this piece is upper end for the grade, even for an MS66, and the color is fantastic. Both sides are covered with a layer of warm rose-gold patina with an accent of lilac over the eagle on the reverse. Sharply defined throughout, the matte-like surfaces show no obvious marks to the unaided eye.
From The Kutasi Collection.(#8865)

Beautiful MS66 1910-D Ten Dollar

3171   1910-D MS66 PCGS. The 1910-D, 1926, and 1932 are the three most commonly encountered ten Indians, and as such have always been the focus of attention for type collectors. The 1910-D has an edge over the other two, however, because of the D-mintmark. This piece would be an unimprovable type coin in terms of color and luster. In terms of technical preservation, it is difficult to imagine a better-preserved 1910-D, but NGC has certified eight pieces finer. This is a "typical" Kutasi coin. That is to say, the color and luster on this piece are consistent with the other coins in his collection. The obverse shows an interplay of rose-gold and lilac patina, while the reverse is primarily reddish in hue with an interesting arc of lilac next to the rim on the right part of that side. Sharply struck throughout and refreshingly clean with no obvious marks on either side.
From The Kutasi Collection.(#8866)

Exceptional MS66 1910-S Ten Dollar, Tied for Finest Known

3172 1910-S MS66 PCGS. The 1910-S ten dollar started out with a large mintage of 811,000 pieces. However, unlike many ten and twenty dollar issues, the 1910-S did not sit around in bags in bank vaults. Almost all the production run appears to have been dropped into circulation. The population data shows what specialists have long known: the 1910-S is common in circulated grades, but it is scarce in mint condition. To be more specific, approximately 900 circulated pieces have been certified by PCGS and NGC. Every grade is represented from AU58 all the way down to a pair of Fine 12 coins. The situation changes dramatically when one looks up the grading ladder from MS60 to the finest coins at the MS66 level. There are 657 pieces that have been certified in Uncirculated condition, and lower grade (60-63) coins are always available for a price. But the herd thins out quickly above that level with only 28 pieces graded MS64. Above MS64 only three Gems have been certified and five graded MS66 by both services. The fact that more MS66s have been graded than MS65s does not mean that more examples are actually known than at the Gem level. This is simply a reflection of how many MS66 coins have been submitted in hopes of gaining an MS67 grade (a hope that is yet unrealized).

Long before population data was looked to for an indication of scarcity, David Akers wrote in 1988 of the 1910-S:

"Despite its high mintage, the 1910-S is a very rare coin in all Mint State grades. Occasionally a specimen in MS-63 or less is available, but it is a highly unusual occurrence when one better than that comes up for sale. In MS-64 condition, the issue is really very rare, and it is my opinion that only about six to eight true gems exist, if that many."

The Kutasi coin is recognized by specialists as one of the two finest known 1910-S tens. Its only real rival appears tobe the Kruthoffer coin, but to our knowledge that coin has not been seen since 1981.

The 1910-S comes in both the satiny and frosted finish. Again, according to Akers "the few really top grade examples of this issue that I have seen have all been much more satiny than frosty." This particular piece has undeniably frosted surfaces with the usual fine-grain finish, a finish that is seen to some degree on all tens from 1908 through 1916. As with all the Kutasi coins, this piece has lovely color. Both sides have a mixture of orange-gold and red-gold patina with a slight bit of lilac interspersed—an obvious sign of originality. The coin is nearly perfect in terms of preservation, with the only (vaguely) noticeable mark placed along the jawline of the Indian.

This is one of the finest if not *the* finest 1910-S eagles known. As such, it presents the collector with a rare (perhaps unique?) opportunity to acquire this condition rarity in the ultimate Uncirculated grade.

Ex: William Thomas Michaels Collection (Stack's, 1/04), lot 3014; the plate coin in the new The Coinage of Augustus Saint-Gaudens as Illustrated by the Phillip Morse Collection.

From The Kutasi Collection.(#8867)

Superb Quality 1911 Ten Dollar, Ex: Morse

3173   1911 MS67 PCGS. The 1911 is one of the more frequently encountered issues in the ten dollar Indian series, but its availability drops off dramatically after the MS64 level. Superb coins are virtually non-existent and are certainly no more available than the 1932 or 1926. Only seven other pieces have been so graded by PCGS with none finer, while NGC has certified seven coins with two finer (11/06).

One of the most interesting stories about the 1911 ten dollar, and one that helps explain its availability in high grade is the discovery of a hoard in the early 1990s. A Pontiac dealership in Ulysses, Kansas had gone out of business after many decades of selling cars and parts. A prospective buyer of the dealership was looking through a dusty storeroom of obsolete parts, and he discovered an old carburetor box that contained 30-40 Mint State 1911 eagles. Apparently the coins had been hidden by the original owner who had long since passed away.

The surfaces of this piece show the fine-grain texture one expects from this date with a generous overlay of yellow-orange frosted mint luster, which flows around each side unimpeded by the abrasions one normally expects from this type. In fact, the only marks we see are a couple of minute, inoffensive ones on the Indian's temple. Simply outstanding quality in this very challenging series. Sharply defined throughout.

Ex: Phillip Morse Collection (Heritage, 11/05), lot 6510, where it realized $46,000.

From The Kutasi Collection.(#8868)

1911-D EAGLE, MS65 PCGS

1911-D EAGLE, MS65 PCGS

Gem 1911-D Ten Dollar, Tied for Finest Known

3174   1911-D MS65 PCGS. The rarity of the 1911-D ten dollar is underscored by the fact that many date and mintmark collectors settle for a Choice AU rather than paying the heavy freight usually required for a high grade Uncirculated coin. And some strong prices have been paid for 1911-D tens in the past! The Norweb coin, which was sold in 1988, realized $132,000, a price that still stands as a record for this date and mintmark. The MS64 in the 1996 RARCOA/Akers sale brought $74,250. And the Heritage 1999 FUN coin, also graded MS64, was hammered at $55,200.

The reason for the scarcity of this issue is twofold. First, only 30,100 pieces were struck, which is the lowest mintage in the entire ten Indian series. Second, it appears that most of the scant mintage was dropped into circulation shortly after striking. Several hundred XF-AU coins have been certified by PCGS and NGC, with almost 150 pieces in AU58, indicating brief circulation for a significant percentage of the few coins struck. The finest 1911-D tens known (certified) are three MS65 coins, inclusive of this Gem. The Price, Duckor, and Michaels collections of ten dollar Indians all lacked a Gem of this date.

One feature that distinguishes this coin from other Mint State 1911-D tens is the sharpness of strike seen on this piece. Often there is slight weakness seen at the juncture of the eagle's wing and breast, as well as on the trailing leg. That is not the case with this example. This is a strongly struck coin in all areas. Also, the color is usually light to medium orange-gold. This piece has deep reddish color and it is evenly dispersed over each side. The surfaces display thick mint frost and pronounced granularity. Strong magnification will be required to find the couple of tiny marks on this coin. One is directly behind the eye of the Indian, appearing like crow's feet; while the other is located in the reverse field below the ST of TRUST.

This is a rare opportunity to acquire this key and major condition rarity to the ten dollar series. The 1911-D is not only one of the rarest issues in this popular series, it is also one of the major rarities of all 20th century United States gold coins. Sometimes the opportunity to acquire a coin of this importance and rarity is as rare as the coin itself. A highlight of the Kutasi Collection.
From The Kutasi Collection.(#8869)

Richly Patinated 1911-S Ten, MS66

3175   1911-S MS66 PCGS. The story of the 1911-S ten dollar is a fascinating one and it is told in its entirety in the new book *The Coinage of Augustus Saint-Gaudens as Illustrated by the Morse Collection.* This date was formerly a major rarity until a Catalan-speaking coin dealer approached Marc Emory in 1979 about 1911-S tens at a coin show in Basel, Switzerland. He eventually purchased 50 examples for $60,000. Most of the coins were high grade and according to Emory, " ... some of which were pristine Gems. All were Mint State with the same light patina over them."

"Light patina" does not accurately describe the color present on this particular coin. Both sides exhibit deep red color with strong underlying mint frost. The surfaces show pronounced granularity which gives a randomly dispersive appearance to the thick mint frost. The only mark of note is located on the reverse, a horizontal abrasion in the field below the final A in AMERICA. Only 10 coins have been certified MS66 by the two major services (eight by PCGS and two by NGC), with none finer (11/06). This is a rare opportunity to acquire one of the finest preserved 1911-S tens known.
From The Kutasi Collection.(#8870)

Lustrous MS66 1912 Eagle

3176   1912 MS66 PCGS. The 1912 has a large mintage of 400,000 pieces and quite a few were preserved in the lower grades of Uncirculated. However, Gem and finer examples are seldom encountered. The Dr. Steven Duckor MS67 coin brought a record-breaking $138,000 when it was sold by Heritage in April 2006. This piece is high-end for the assigned grade and exhibits a strong strike throughout with rich, frosted mint luster. The surfaces show the usual matte-like finish that is seen on all gold from this period, and the color is a deep, almost brown-gold. All of these characteristics combine to make the 1912 an appealing choice for type purposes, even though it is slightly better than the most frequently seen ten Indians. A couple of random luster scrapes are seen in the fields, and the only mentionable mark is located in the upper reverse field just to the right of the head of the eagle. Population: 7 in 66, 1 finer (11/06).
From The Kutasi Collection.(#8871)

Splendid MS65 1912-S Ten Dollar

3177   1912-S MS65 PCGS. Like most of the S-mints from this decade, the 1912-S is an issue that is rarely seen in grades above MS64, and even then not that often. In Gem condition a mere 11 coins have been certified with three finer (11/06). The reason is not one of mintage, as 300,000 pieces were struck. Rather, most 1912-S eagles are weakly struck and luster is below average, two attributes that prevent even the cleanest examples from high grades. This coin has a strong strike on each side and the mint luster is comparable to other S-mints in the series. Both sides are covered with rich, deep reddish-gold color and the only (slightly) noticeable mark is located in the left obverse field out from the nose. Only 11 Gems have been certified by PCGS and NGC combined with a mere three pieces finer (11/06). An underrated and often misunderstood issue which typically lacks the eye appeal and attractiveness of other issues in the series.
From The Kutasi Collection.(#8872)

Lovely, Lustrous MS66 1913 Ten Dollar

3178   1913 MS66 PCGS. While common enough in lower grades, enough so to be used for type purposes, the 1913 is a condition rarity in MS66 condition. The only graded MS67 example from the Dr. Steven Duckor collection realized $126,500 when it was sold by Heritage in April 2006. A small hoard of about 20 pieces was discovered in an old tavern in Niagara Falls, New York behind the bar-back. This discovery significantly increased the number of high grade 1913 twenties available to collectors of high grade 20th century gold. John Kutasi discovered this coin while searching through gold coin registry sets on the internet and contacted the owner via email. As a result, this piece was acquired for the Kutasi Collection directly from another collector in the U.K. This is a wonderful example that has radiant mint luster and rich orange-gold color. The surfaces are remarkably clean, even for an MS66 coin. The only marks we see that might be useful for tracing the pedigree of this coin in the future are located in the field below the M in UNUM—but then, we are looking with a strong magnifier and these may not be visible in older catalogs.
Ex: David Hall Rare Coins; Peter Gamble (collector in the U.K.). From The Kutasi Collection.(#8873)

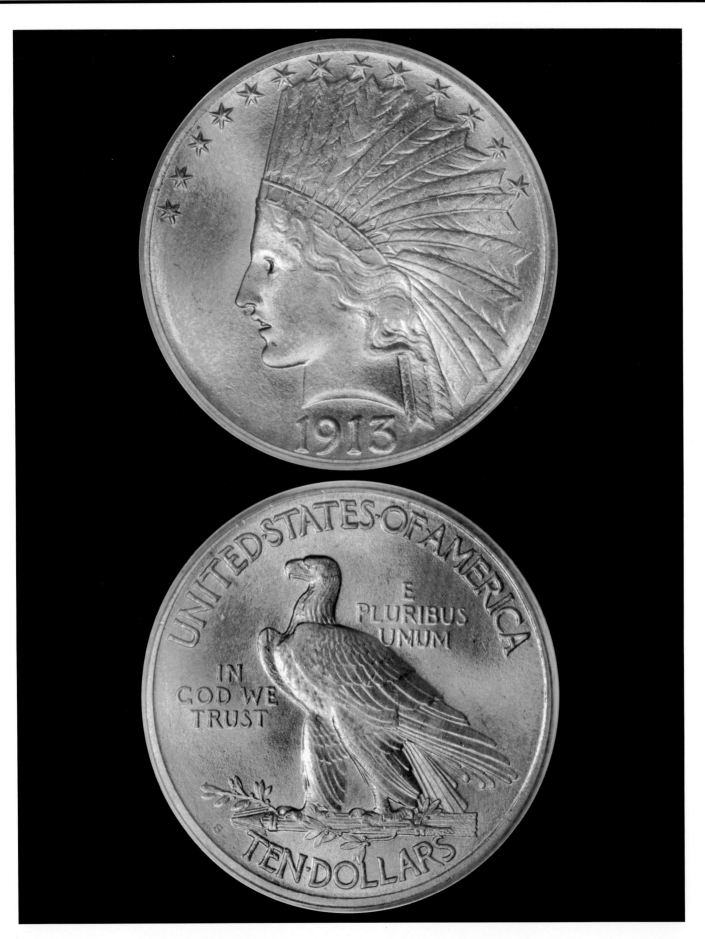

1913-S Ten Dollar, MS66, A Premier Rarity
in the Ten Dollar Indian Series

3179   1913-S MS66 PCGS. The first two sentences from the Garrett-Guth *Gold Encyclopedia* tell the story of high grade 1913-S eagles: "The 1913-S eagle was once the undisputed key to the series. Since the advent of certification, however, this premier condition rarity has been nudged out of top place by the 1911-D issue." For most collectors of this series, the issue of which issue is rarer is comparable to debating about how many angels can dance on the head of a pin. High grade examples are so rare of both that mind-boggling prices have been realized at public auction in recent years. As long ago as 1989, an MS65 brought $198,000. The last time an MS66 was sold was in 2000 in a Bowers sale, and that coin realized $71,300. Pricing data is obviously scarce and difficult for this rarely seen issue; however, a pair of MS67 coins (the only two certified MS67 examples) brought $200,000 and $143,750 via a Heritage private sale (2005) and Stack's (1/2004) auction respectively.

Only 66,000 pieces were produced of the 1913-S and apparently a substantial percentage of that mintage was dropped into circulation as most of the coins known today are in VF to Choice AU condition. Lower-end Uncirculated coins are challenging in the absolute sense with only 100 or so pieces extant today in the MS60-62 grade range. A mere 24 coins have been certified in MS63, and this slight number gives one a sense of the rarity of the 1913-S in even higher grades. Such pieces are rarely seen, and when they available they are highlight coins in whatever auction in which they are offered.

The present specimen was formerly one of two NGC coins graded MS67 maintained in the current population reports and which was last sold by Heritage to John Kutasi via the above-mentioned private sale for $200,000 in April 2005. It is now the sole MS66 example graded by PCGS. The only other known NGC MS67 example resides in the collection of an Eastern Prominent collector. It is also important to note that this date was conspicuously absent in Gem grades from other notable ten dollar Indian collections such as Price, Duckor, and Kruthoffer, which had MS63 examples of this key date.

The surfaces show a lovely overlay of light orange-gold color with a mixture of lilac on the reverse. Each side is evenly covered with matte-like granularity with an overlay of soft, frosted mint luster. The only mark of note is a short, shallow check-mark near the rim at 7 o'clock on the obverse.

Once again quoting from the Garrett-Guth reference: "Any Indian Head eagle collection would be truly defined by the presence of both a 1913-S and a 1911-D issue." This is a colossal ten dollar Indian whose condition would be noteworthy even if it were dated 1932. The fact it is one of the rarest and most famous issues of this popular series will make this a coin that will be remembered for many years to come. *Used as the plate coin in* The Coinage of Augustus Saint-Gaudens as Illustrated by the Phillip Morse Collection. *From The Kutasi Collection.*(#8874)

One of the Finest Known
1914 Tens, MS66 PCGS

3180   1914 MS66 PCGS. Ex: Duckor. Along with the 1909, the 1914 is one of the scarcest of the Philadelphia Mint regular issues of the Indian Head ten dollar type. Gold specialist David Akers, in his May 1998 catalog of the *Dr. Thaine B. Price Collection,* wrote: "For many years, this issue was widely considered to be a rather underrated date. However, recently a number of decent quality mint state specimens have appeared on the market reducing this date's rarity status somewhat. Even so, the 1914 is still the second rarest Philadelphia Mint eagle from 1908-1915, exceeded only by the considerably more rare 1909."

Judging by the population reports, the 1914 is not that difficult to obtain in the lesser Mint State grades. Around 1,500 examples have been certified by PCGS and NGC combined in grades MS60 to MS63. Near-Gems, with fewer than 250 certified specimens, become more elusive, and full Gems, with about 60 pieces seen, are quite scarce. MS66 and MS67 coins, with a current certified population of 18 and three, respectively, are virtually unobtainable. This coin set a new record for the date and mintmark when it was sold in April 2006 and realized $40,250.

The 1914 eagle in this lot possesses the typically strong luster characteristics with thick mint frost. Highly attractive peach-gold patina displays occasional blushes of deeper orange, and is imbued with subtle traces of light green. The design elements are exquisitely brought up, including nice definition on the hair near the Indian's ear. A tiny mark on the nose and a couple of more on the cheekbone identify the coin. Population: 7 in 66, 2 finer (11/06).
From The Kutasi Collection.(#8875)

Impressive MS66 1914-D Ten Dollar

3181   1914-D MS66 PCGS. The 1914-D is generally considered the second most-available D-mint ten dollar Indian. The 1910-D, of course, is the most common D-mint, but there is a significant difference between the two at the high end of the grading spectrum. At the MS64 and MS65 levels, the '14-D is about four times scarcer than the '10-D. At the MS66 level only 15 coins have been certified with nine finer (11/06). The pronounced granularity on both sides of this piece is overlaid with bright, satiny mint luster. The surfaces are exceptionally well preserved, as one would expect from an MS66, with no obvious or mentionable marks on either side. As with most of the coins in the Kutasi Collection, this piece shows memorable color. Each side has subtle pinkish-rose patina that is interspersed with lilac on the reverse. The ever-increasing popularity and demand for this series is evidenced by the realization of $109,250 for the Dr. Steven Duckor MS67 example of this date sold by Heritage in April 2006.

From The Kutasi Collection.(#8876)

Lustrous Gem 1914-S Ten Dollar Indian

3182   1914-S MS65 PCGS. The extreme rarity of the 1914-S in the better grades of Uncirculated is well known to specialists and is extensively discussed in the write-up for the MS66 following. Suffice it to say that fewer than two dozen Gems have been certified by the two major services. When the MS66 (Lot 3183) was sold in June 2006, the cataloger for ANR noted "...examples that appeared in such important collections as Thaine Price, where the specimen was catalogued as Choice Mint State, and that of William Thomas Michaels whose collection contained a MS-65, graded by NGC. Going back to the Eliasberg and Norweb Collections, it is significant to note that the date was represented in both cabinets by pieces graded AU-50!" All these collections are noted for high quality coins, and it is a significant offering for the collector of ten dollar Indians that an MS65 and an MS66 are offered in the same sale.

This piece has the same frosted mint luster and matte-like surfaces as the MS66. The striking details are similar as well. The main difference between the two is the presence of several small abrasions (magnification required) that are scattered over each side of this piece. Rich, even, deep orange-gold color completes the description of this important, key issue in the ten Indian series.

From The Kutasi Collection.(#8877)

Exceptional MS66 1914-S Ten Dollar, Tied for Second Finest Known

3183   1914-S MS66 PCGS. As with many ten and twenty dollar gold pieces of the Saint-Gaudens design, the original mintage does not tell the collector much about the rarity of a particular issue. In the case of the 1914-S ten, the mintage was 208,000 pieces. Certainly a sufficient number to provide collectors with numerous high grade examples, or so one would think. However, probably no more than 1,000 examples are known today, most of which are spread through the XF to MS63 grades. It is in MS64 and better condition that the 1914-S shines as one of the premier condition rarities in the series. The always-quotable David Akers commented about the condition rarity of the 1914-S in the Thaine Price (1998) catalog: "Above the Choice level, the 1914-S is one of the most important condition rarities of the series, much more rare than the 1908-S, 1909-S, 1911-S, 1912-S and 1916-S ..." We would add to his comparison to the other S-mints, that the 1914-S is also scarcer than the D-mints and all the Philadelphia issues from 1908-1915. The 1914-S is indeed among the most undervalued issues in the series, along with the 1912-S and the 1915-S. It is ironic that the 1930-S carries a much higher valuation than these three S-mints, even though the surviving number of Gems of the 1930-S is significantly higher.

In Gem condition, only 22 pieces have been certified by the two major services. In MS66 a mere four coins have been graded, and there is a single, tantalizing NGC MS67 piece that has not been seen in many years. The surfaces of this coin are nearly perfect. The last time it appeared in public auction (June of last year), the cataloger noted a small identifying mark located in the eagle's wing feathers below the M in UNUM. In addition to being exceptionally clean, the surfaces show strong mint frost over a matte-like finish. As with most 1914-S tens, the color on this piece is exceptional, and both sides exude a rich orange-gold color.

Ex: Lake Michigan and Springdale Collections (ANR, 6/06), lot 2641, where it brought $253,000.

From The Kutasi Collection.(#8877)

Intensely Lustrous MS66 1915 Ten Dollar

3184   1915 MS66 PCGS. The 1915 is among the more available issues in the ten dollar Indian series in Uncirculated grades. Among P-mint dates, it is much scarcer than the 1932 and 1926, and it is also scarcer than the 1907 No Periods, 1908 With Motto, and 1911. When considered as a type coin, the 1915 presents the collector with new challenges. Because it has granular surfaces, as do all tens struck from 1908 through 1916, eye appeal can be a problem because of the dispersive effect of the matte-like finish. However, this piece is notable for its bright mint frost that overpowers the pronounced granularity seen over both obverse and reverse. Sharply struck in most areas, the only trace of softness is on the fore part of the eagle's wing. The coin has distinctive color with an interplay of orange-gold, yellow-gold, and lilac over each side. Despite its common status in lower grades, the 1915 is seldom offered in MS66 condition with only 22 other pieces graded as such by both PCGS and NGC combined, and five finer (11/06).
From The Kutasi Collection.(#8878)

One of the Finest Known 1915-S Tens, MS65 PCGS, Ex: Price, Thomas

3185   1915-S MS65 PCGS. The 1915-S is an absolute as well as a condition rarity in the ten dollar Indian series. Only 59,000 pieces were struck, and apparently few were shipped overseas as no hoards are mentioned in the literature and so few Uncirculated pieces known. Probably fewer than 200 pieces are known today in all grades of Uncirculated, with the vast majority of these graded MS63 or less. At the Gem level, only seven other coins have been certified with four in higher grades (11/06).

The new *The Coinage of Augustus Saint-Gaudens as Illustrated by the Morse Collection* mentions a couple of the finest examples of this issue that are known, and indicates the price levels the 1915-S can attain when conditions are right: "The finest example certified to date is an NGC MS67, a coin that has not been offered at public auction (at that grade) that we are aware of. The two 1915-S tens that have realized the highest price at public auction were both sold in 1989. Superior sold a PCGS MS65 that brought $198,000, and Heritage sold a PCGS MS66 later that same year, but after the 1989 investor-crazed market had softened. The latter coin realized $192,500."

This is a particularly clean and attractive example. It is also a coin that has been an integral part of three major collections of ten Indians. The surfaces have pronounced granularity (not always the case on 1915-S tens) with satiny mint luster. Both sides exhibit lovely reddish-gold color with occasional flecks of lilac interspersed. The only identifiers that can be reliably used for pedigree purposes are a short horizontal mark below the eye on the obverse, and a small alloy stain at 5 o'clock on that same side.

Ex: Thaine Price Collection (Akers, 5/98), lot 65; William Michael Thomas (Stack's, 1/04), lot 3026.
From The Kutasi Collection.(#8879)

Exceptional MS66 PCGS
1916-S Ten Dollar

3186   1916-S MS66 PCGS. It is interesting that both the ten and twenty dollar issues of the 1916-S were hoarded and those hoard coins are responsible for the majority of high grade examples known today. Of course, the difference between the two hoards is that some of the tens were discovered in Beverly Hills, while a bag of the twenties turned up in El Salvador. Most of the hoard coins of the tens display muted luster for some reason, which is one reason we believe this piece is not a hoard piece. The luster is radiant with dramatic rose and lilac iridescence on each side. Another reason it does not appear to be a hoard piece is the exceptionally high grade, which in large part is derived from the lack of abrasions on each side. The strike is typical for the issue with some softness apparent on the fore part of the eagle's wing and also on the right (facing) claw. All S-mint ten dollar Indians are rare in the highest grade and the 1916-S is no exception, which is supported by the population data. An MS66 example was last offered in the Heritage sale of the Phillip Morse collection in November 2005 where it realized $48,875. Population: 5 in 66, 2 finer (11/06).
From The Kutasi Collection.(#8880)

Exceptional MS66 1920-S Ten Dollar, Tied for Second Finest Known

3187 1920-S MS66 PCGS. This year marked the first production of gold coinage since 1916. From the time 126,500 eagles were struck at the San Francisco Mint in 1920, they were considered one of the rarest of all 20th century ten dollar gold coins. Evidently, nearly all were exported in commercial trade, or held in Treasury vaults and eventually melted in the 1930s. No hoards have ever turned up and the coin remains very rare to this day.

T. Louis Comparette, curator of the Philadelphia Mint coin collection, was an important conduit of new coins for the Connecticut State Library's Mitchelson Collection and a few other institutions. Although specimens struck in Philadelphia were usually available with little difficulty, pieces from the other mints were available only from the pyx coins reserved for use of the Annual Assay Commission. (Collectors could usually purchase issued coins directly from each mint, but the quality of specimens was often well below the pyx coins.) On March 1, 1921, Comparette sent George Godard, the Connecticut State Librarian, two of the San Francisco eagles.

> "Here are two eagles struck at the San Francisco Mint in 1920. With some difficulty I was able to secure four specimens from the pyx, of which I send you these, one for your collections, the other for Sen. Hall, whose interests I am still willing to assist, though he will not answer my letters."

One of these was acquired by Godard from the estate of Connecticut State Senator William Henry Hall, whose personal collection included the duplicates sent by Comparette. It was sold by Stack's with Godard's personal collection in 1982. The other remains in the Mitchelson Collection. The Smithsonian National Numismatic Collection includes an example that was likely a third coin saved from the pyx. The fact that individual specimens of this issue are so easily traced underscores the absolute rarity of the 1920-S. This particular coin last appeared in the extraordinary collection of ten dollar Indians that was assembled by William Thomas Michaels. That set was sold in January 2004. The cataloger for Stack's wrote an insightful commentary on the 1920-S:

> "Although 126,500 coins of this date are reported to have been struck, it is quite evident that nearly all were melted before ever leaving the Mint. Unlike other key dates in this series such as the 1930 'S' and 1933 that, when available, are almost always encountered in Mint State, this date is found in all grades. The fact that most known survivors range in condition from Very Fine to Choice Brilliant Uncirculated only intensifies the desirability of the small number of Gem quality specimens extant."

This wide range of grades of availability (or unavailability as the case is more apt to be) points to a curious duality that is alluded to in the Stack's description. That is, an effort was made to release the 1920-S into circulation, as indicated by the 49 coins certified by PCGS and NGC in VF30 to AU58 grades. Apparently, what need there was for ten dollar coins that had not been produced since 1916, was soon met and the remainder were eventually melted. Breen speculates that the varying amount of bagmarks found on most 1920-S tens attests to "their long residence in bank cash reserves." Thus, the 1920-S is both an absolute and condition rarity.

Most of the known 1920-S tens show weakness of strike on the RTY of LIBERTY, but this is more of a tendency than an absolute diagnostic. This piece shows a full R but TY is not visible. What is an absolute, however, is weakness on the trailing leg of the eagle. Otherwise, the surfaces show the usual frosty mint luster that is always seen on mint examples of this rarity. The surfaces are remarkably clean, as one would expect for an MS66, with a tiny planchet flake on the cheek of Liberty and another at the top of the eagle's trailing leg—the most notable pedigree identifiers on this piece. The color on this coin is nothing short of extraordinary. Each side shows an intermixture of deep rose-gold and lilac patina that adds significantly to the overall eye appeal of this exceptionally well preserved coin. Only one other piece has been certified as MS66, an NGC coin, and only one 1920-S is finer, a PCGS MS67, presently in the collection of Dr. Steven Duckor. This piece represents an opportunity for the advanced collector to add this key issue to a collection of ten dollar Indians. Rarely are such coins available in any condition, and at the MS66 level this piece is tied for second finest known.

Ex: William Thomas Michaels Collection (Stack's, 1/04), lot 3028, where it brought $241,500.

From The Kutasi Collection.(#8881)

Clean, Lustrous MS66 1926 Ten Dollar

3188   1926 MS66 PCGS. While the 1926 is widely recognized as the second most common ten Indian, this is an uncommonly fine example. As a rule, the 1926 is found with excellent luster but heavy bagmarks limit most coins to the MS63-64 grade range. Literally thousands of pieces are available in those grades, but the numbers known drops sharply at the MS65 level to 700 or so. But the really precipitous decline is seen at the next grade level, that of the present piece, where only eight coins have been certified by PCGS and 35 by NGC. It is also worthy of note that there are no coins graded finer at either of the major services. As pointed out in *The Coinage of Augustus Saint-Gaudens as Illustrated by the Morse Collection,* " ... there is no universally recognized, single-finest example of the 1926." If one measures finest known by the highest price an MS66 has brought, then that honor goes to the coin that sold for $14,950 in Heritage's September 2003 Long Beach Sale.

This particular piece is especially clean for the grade. The only marks are hidden in the upper feathers of the headdress. Otherwise, the surfaces are exceptionally clean and show what we refer to as "Kutasi color," that is, an original, untampered coin with rich reddish patina and varying amounts of lilac interspersed, especially in the recesses and in the fields. Well defined throughout. This is surely one of the finest 1926 tens known, a fact that will undoubtedly be borne out by the price it realizes.
From The Kutasi Collection.(#8882)

Lustrous, Beautifully Patinated
Gem 1930-S Ten Dollar

3189   1930-S MS65 PCGS. The mintage of the 1930-S ten was sufficient that one would think it would be more available than it actually is. But this issue repeats the familiar pattern in the Saint-Gaudens' designed ten and twenty dollar series of relatively high mintage and low availability. This, of course, is because of the widespread meltings from the 1930s. This was so extensive that today probably no more than 125-140 pieces are known in all grades. As further proof of the melting of this issue, a glance at the population figures from PCGS and NGC shows that no more than a handful of coins are lightly circulated, thus this issue was probably never released into the channels of commerce. With most of the known 1930-S tens in Uncirculated grades, this absolute rarity then becomes a condition rarity also. Only 27 pieces have been certified as MS65 by PCGS and NGC, with five in MS66, and three in MS67.

The existence and possible existence of hoards is always an interesting topic of discussion in the ten and twenty dollar series. One of the most intriguing bits of speculation in Breen's *Encyclopedia* involves a story about the 1930-S ten: "For some decades, one 1930-S turned up in the San Francisco area every three years, probably from a single roll." If Breen's speculation was correct, by now the original supply would be exhausted.

This is a memorable example that has rich, frosted mint luster with an even layer of reddish-golden patina. With magnification, one can see slight traces of lilac over the highpoints. Most easily identifiable as the Kutasi coin by the presence of a shallow, diagonal mark in the field out from the left, forward curve of the eagle's wing.

Used as the plate coin in the new The Coinage of Augustus Saint-Gaudens as Illustrated by the Morse Collection.

From The Kutasi Collection.(#8883)

Lustrous MS66 1932 Indian Ten

3190   1932 MS66 PCGS. As the most frequently seen ten dollar Indian, there are literally thousands of coins available from MS60 to MS65 condition. Far fewer examples are known at the MS66 level, primarily because of what Akers terms "unsightly surface 'cuts' that seem heavier than typical bagmarks." Probably around 200 coins are known at the MS66 level, far fewer than the number of collectors of high grade 20th century gold type. Like the 1926, there is no singular, finest-known 1932 ten dollar. However, if one judges by the price realized at public auction, then the still-reigning champion is the Thaine Price coin that was described as "nearly flawless" and sold in May 1998 for $27,000.

This is a lovely, well struck coin that exhibits rich, even reddish-gold color and thick, swirling mint frost. Undoubtedly one of the finest 1932 tens known and worthy of inclusion in another high grade set.

From The Kutasi Collection.(#8884)

1933 EAGLE, MS65 PCGS

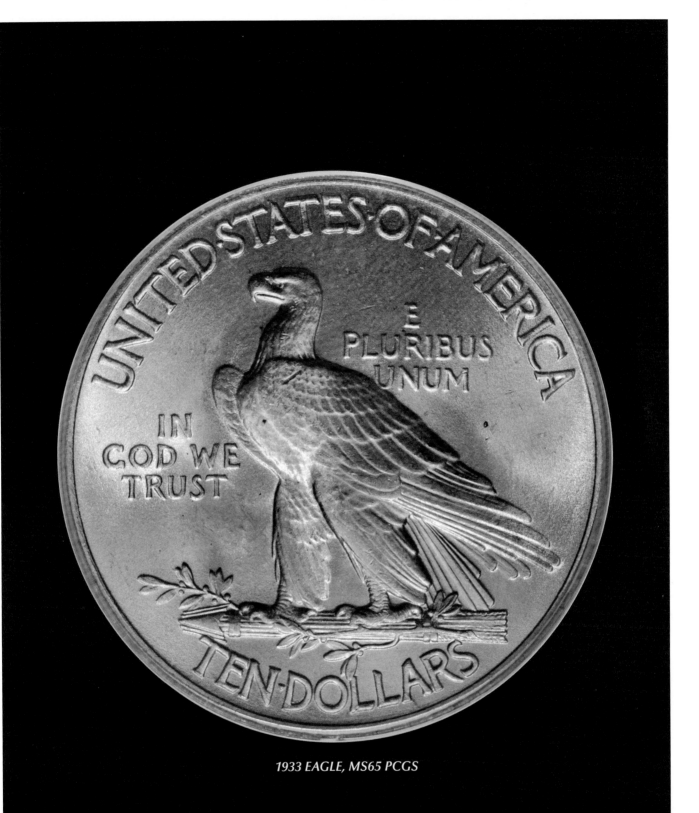

1933 EAGLE, MS65 PCGS

Memorable MS65 1933 Ten Dollar

3191   1933 MS65 PCGS. The 1933 eagle had a sizeable mintage of 312,500 pieces. All were struck in January and February 1933, and most pieces were subsequently melted after the Presidential order. Some of those coins—perhaps numbering three or four dozen pieces—were legally released through regular channels at that time. About 30 survivors were uncovered in an East Coast hoard in 1952, and a few others have since turned up in French and Swiss banks. The 1933 eagle, however, is still among the rarest Indian tens in all grades. The new and indispensable Garrett-Guth gold *Encyclopedia* opines that "Owning an example of this date is certainly one of the highlights of any numismatic collection, and a feat precious few collectors can ever hope to accomplish." A total of only 34 Mint State coins have been graded at NGC and PCGS combined. The present MS65 coin is tied with seven other MS65 pieces at PCGS, with no examples finer. At NGC, there are only three Gems certified, and one piece finer (11/06).

While Akers states that some 1933 tens have a satiny finish, the three examples in this sale all have decidedly frosted mint luster. This piece has even reddish-gold coloration, and the surfaces are remarkably clean even for a Gem. The striking details are also strong throughout. While there are many notable, rare, and high grade coins in the Kutasi Collection, this 1933 ten dollar will certainly be one of the, if not *the* most memorable coin in this spectacular group.
From The Kutasi Collection.(#8885)

Reflective MS62 1872-S Double Eagle, Ex: Bass

3192   1872-S MS62 PCGS. Bowers, in *A Guide Book of Double Eagle Gold Coins* states that the highest auction price ever paid for a 1872-S double eagle was $8,625, for lot 840 of the May, 2000 Harry W. Bass, Jr. Collection auction. We are unaware of any subsequent sales results that would challenge this record, which was established by this very coin. It was described at that time as:

> "Reflective, mirrored fields and lustrous orange-gold devices provide an attractive cameo effect. Light surface marks are noted on both obverse and reverse. A very rare issue in high grades, with nearly all of the 20 to 30 Mint State survivors just MS60 in quality. Incredibly, the market value of this piece is only in the range of a couple of thousand dollars. Talk about potential!"

Six and a half years later, PCGS has certified a total of 38 coins of the date in Mint State grades, and still none are finer than this piece. It is fully prooflike, although PCGS does not certify gold coins as such. It is also blessed with a strong strike for the issue, with full detail showing on all stars, although Liberty's hair is flat, as often found. Population: 3 in 62, 0 finer (11/06).
Ex: Parke-Bernet (5/68), lot 45; Harry W. Bass, Jr. Collection (Bowers and Merena, 5/00), lot 840.
From The Kutasi Collection.(#8965)

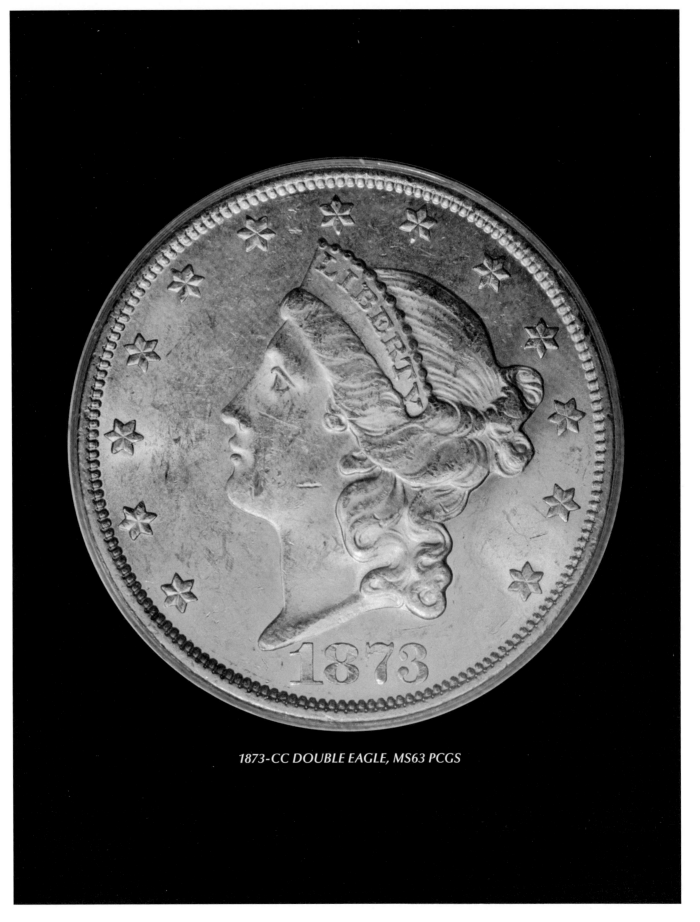

1873-CC DOUBLE EAGLE, MS63 PCGS

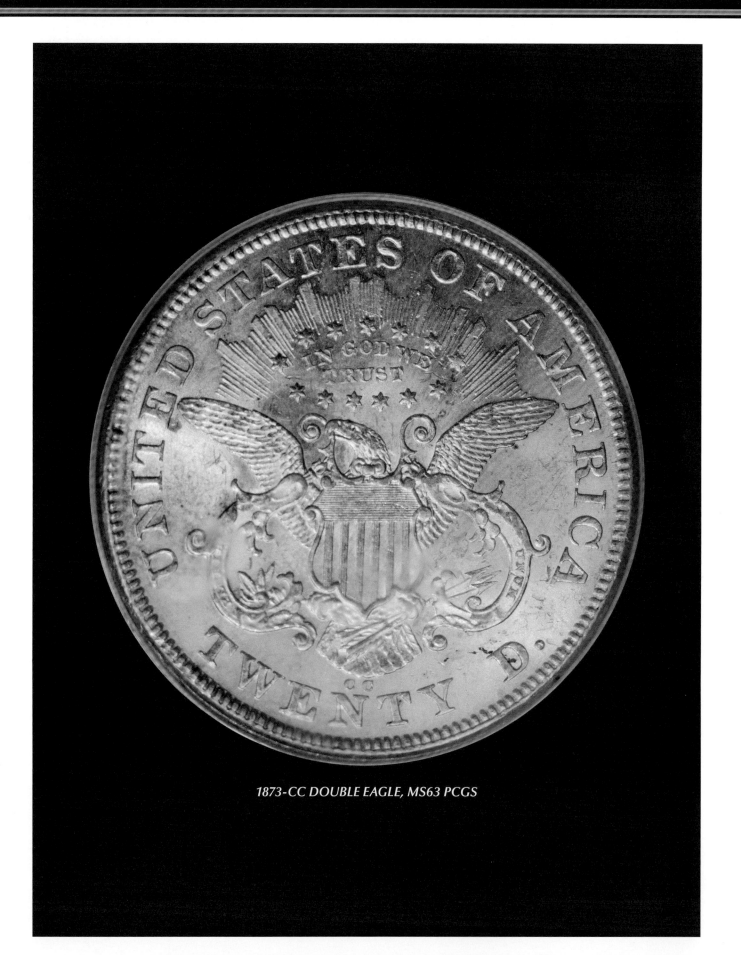

1873-CC DOUBLE EAGLE, MS63 PCGS

Finest Certified 1873-CC Double Eagle MS63

3193   1873-CC MS63 PCGS. Ex: Texas Collection. The ultra-rare 1870-CC Double Eagle garners more headlines, but the other Carson City issues from the early 1870s are also very difficult. Mintages reached 26,900 pieces in 1872, then fell slightly to 22,410 pieces in 1873. It was not until the 1874-CC that production achieved six figures, and it is the 1874-CC to 1876-CC issues that usually represents the Type Two design within Carson City type sets.

The Philadelphia Mint introduced the Open 3 logotype early in the 1873, as a result of complaints that the Closed 3 too closely resembled the digit 8 to the naked eye. While the 1873 Open 3 Twenties are common relative to their Open 3 counterparts, the opposite is the case with the 1873-S, since the new dies had to journey from Philadelphia to San Francisco before they could be put into production. The new logotype dies must have arrived in Carson City late in the year or not at all, as all known 1873-CC Twenties feature a Closed 3.

A well struck piece, this lovely Double Eagle has vibrant cartwheel luster, and relevant blemishes are limited to a trio of separated marks on the cheek. The reverse rim near 7 o'clock is moderately abraded, however, this is far from the focal point of the coin. Limited in mintage to begin with, Carson City Twenties were regarded strictly as bullion in the old west, and it is nearly miraculous for a piece to have been set aside upon issue and never circulated. Gold coins were not collected by mintmark until the 20th century.

Although it is hard to find in all grades, the 1873-CC is extremely rare in Mint State. The importance of this coin to the devoted Carson City or Double Eagle specialist cannot be exaggerated. In his 2001 reference *Gold Coins of the Carson City Mint,* noted branch mint gold specialist Douglas Winter lists the present piece as #1 in his condition census for the 1873-CC. Population: 1 in 63, 0 finer (11/06).
From The Kutasi Collection.(#8968)

Appealing MS63 1875 Double Eagle

3194   1875 MS63 PCGS. The double eagle of 1875 is the only common-date gold coin in a year that is legendary for its gold rarities, some of them proof-only issues. Business strikes of this date were produced to the extent of more than 295,000 pieces. The double eagle is readily available up to and including Mint State pieces. The present piece offers somewhat scuffy but appealing surfaces, with deep orange-gold coloration and considerable luster. While the population in MS63 is nearly four dozen pieces, only three coins at that service have been graded finer (11/06).
From The Kutasi Collection.(#8973)

Richly Colored 1875-CC Twenty MS63

3195   1875-CC MS63 PCGS. The 1874-CC and 1875-CC double eagle issues were produced to the extent of more than 100,000 pieces each, so that examples are available up to the lower Mint State grades. The 1874-CC is seldom seen above MS60, however, and the 1875-CC is elusive above MS61. In MS63, NGC and PCGS combined have certified only about four dozen coins, almost assuredly including numerous duplications. This richly colored example offers orange-gold surfaces with some field-device contrast, good eye appeal, and few singular abrasions. A nice one for the Carson City aficionados.
From The Kutasi Collection.(#8974)

Conditionally Unsurpassable
1877 Twenty MS64

3196   1877 MS64 PCGS. Many of the Liberty Head double eagles from this era are considered to be common dates, and are available in all grades through the lowest Mint State grade levels. Few have survived in higher Mint State grades, a characteristic that is true for even the most common of issues. This 1877 issue is a typical example. The mintage of 397,670 coins is actually rather significant for these coins, especially from the Philadelphia Mint. Nearly all entered commerce, and today only 300 Mint State examples have been certified by PCGS. From that total, 286 have received grades from MS60 to MS62, another 13 coins have been graded MS63, and this solitary example has been certified at MS64. (The other major grading service, NGC, has likewise encapsulated just one MS64 and none finer.)

Known for its tendency for flashiness and as the first year of the Type Three design, this exceptional 1877 double eagle certainly lives up to its reputation. Both sides exhibit a dazzling, semi-reflective appearance and frosty features beneath a layer of reddish-orange patina that is enhanced by lime-green accents in the fields and near the peripheries. Scattered facial marks and a trio of reeding marks on Liberty's neck separate this piece from potential Gem status. Population: 1 in 64, 0 finer (11/06).

From The Kutasi Collection.(#8982)

Lustrous MS62 1877-CC Twenty,
Among Finest Graded

3197   1877-CC MS62 PCGS. As one may readily infer from the 'mingy' emission of only 42,565 pieces, the 1877-CC double eagle is a key to the Type Three issues. In all grades this is an elusive coin. This issue is essentially unknown in a grade finer than MS62, as PCGS has graded five such pieces, with four more at NGC and none finer at either service (11/06). This example boasts lustrous orange-gold surfaces with a bit of light smoke-gray patina and some light scuffs and abrasions consistent with the grade and some bag storage. Pleasing luster emanates from each side, and considerable eye appeal remains.

From The Kutasi Collection.(#8983)

Lustrous MS63 1877-S Double Eagle

3198   1877-S MS63 PCGS. Because of the bountiful mintage of 1.735 million pieces, this issue is available in all grades, up through a few MS64 pieces. The present example appears quite pleasing and high-end for the Select grade, with brilliant cartwheel luster, pretty apricot-gold color and minimally abraded surfaces. The strike is well executed, save for a bit of weakness on the highpoint hair below Liberty's coronet, but the superb, coruscating luster is this coin's most notable hallmark. PCGS has certified 19 examples in MS63, with three coins finer (11/06).
From The Kutasi Collection.(#8984)

Bright 1878 Twenty, MS63 PCGS

3199   1878 MS63 PCGS. Bright luster shines from the orange-gold surfaces of this appealing double eagle, which retains a good deal of mint frost on the devices. The surfaces show a few small abrasions, in line with the grade, and hint ever so slightly at being prooflike. A couple of alloy spots are noted on the reverse.
From The Kutasi Collection.(#8985)

Attractive 1879-S Double Eagle MS61 PCGS

3201   1879-S MS61 PCGS. Bright swirling luster and deeper-than-usual coloration are the most immediately noteworthy attributes of this appealing Mint State example. The striking details are crisp and clear on virtually every design element. Numerous minor abrasions are noted that define the grade.
From The Kutasi Collection.(#8991)

Lustrous MS61 1880-S Twenty Dollars

3202   1880-S MS61 PCGS. Cartwheel luster sweeps the apricot-gold fields, and the strike is crisp throughout. Small marks are scattered, as expected of the MS61 grade. The 1880-S is surprising elusive in Uncirculated grades, and PCGS has only certified four pieces above MS62 (11/06).
From The Kutasi Collection.(#8993)

Select Mint State 1879 Twenty

3200   1879 MS63 PCGS. This P-mint double eagle issue is not at all common, but pieces are available in all grades up to MS62, with finer pieces quite elusive. The present example offers somewhat muted luster with amber-gold coloration, some light field haze, and a couple of small areas of lighter coloration on the reverse. This issue was formerly considered quite rare, but repatriations of overseas hoards have replenished the supply. PCGS has certified only a half-dozen pieces in MS63, with none finer (11/06). NGC adds another four coins in MS63, but again there are none finer at that service.
From The Kutasi Collection.(#8988)

Finest Certified 1881
Double Eagle MS61

3203   1881 MS61 PCGS. The 1881 double eagle commences what David Akers refers to as a "run of seven ultra low mintage issues from the Philadelphia Mint." Business strike production of a mere 2,199 pieces provides the first ingredient for rarity and the fact that few were spared from the ravages of commerce secures its place among the most challenging Liberty twenties. Of the 35-40 pieces believed to survive, only a small handful qualifies as Mint State. Although Heritage Signature Auctions have long been a prime source of rare date gold, nearly six years lapsed between the only other two Uncirculated we have offered, a PCGS MS60 in our 1998 ANA Sale (which may now reside in an MS61 holder since the current combined MS60 population is zero) and a PCGS MS61 selling in our June 2004 Long Beach Sale for $57,500.

This important Uncirculated representative is a bit more reflective than the other two Mint State pieces sold over the past decade, not surprising since so few 1881 twenties were originally produced. Abrasions are fairly plentiful in the obverse fields, but are not particularly bothersome on the portrait and are a bit less numerous and even distributed over the reverse. With interest in "blue chip" gold coins such as this at an all-time high, we feel confident that this low mintage gold rarity in unsurpassable condition could reach a record price level. Population: 2 in 61, 0 finer (11/06).
From The Kutasi Collection.(#8994)

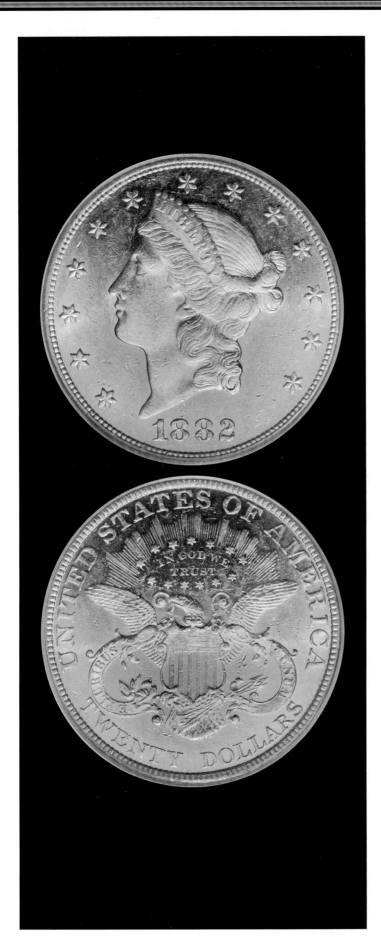

Extremely Rare Uncirculated
1882 Double Eagle

3204 1882 MS60 PCGS. Ex: Dr. Barry Southerland Collection. Last offered (but not sold) at public auction in our August, 2000 Philadelphia Sale as lot 7471. We quote in part from that description, updating where necessary: "First introduced in 1849, Longacre's Liberty motif would grace the double eagle through 1907. This long-lived series has numerous scarce deliveries and several legendary rarities among its business strike issues. The latter include the 1854-O, 1856-O, 1861 Paquet, 1870-CC, 1881, 1885, and 1886. With a total original mintage of only 630 pieces, the 1882 not also belongs in the same category as these other issues, but it surpasses all of them in terms of rarity with the exception of the 1861 Paquet. Unlike the 1881, the 1882 is more difficult to locate in business strike format. There are perhaps 13-15 extant proofs from an original delivery of 59 specimens, but Akers places the total number of business strike survivors at no more than 12 coins....

According to Breen (1977 and 1988), the Philadelphia Mint used a single pair of dies to produce its 571 business strike and 59 proof 1882 double eagles. Since most, if not all of the business strikes are fully prooflike and some of the proofs have been impaired from either circulation or mishandling, the line between the two deliveries can become blurry. For example, Akers (1982) states: "There is also one known [Uncirculated 1882 double eagle] and that coin is really something. By the most conservative grading standards it is a true Gem...or possibly even a bit better." Since we are confident that Akers could not have been referring to the present example, he may have mistaken a well preserved proof for a Gem BU survivor. Still, we must also allow for the possibility that Akers was referring to a coin that has since remained uncertified, perhaps tucked away in the collection of a little known specialist.

The potential confusion that surrounds this issue notwithstanding, we are confident that this Uncirculated example will garner all of the accolades that its low mintage and poor rate of survival deserve. This is a fully prooflike example whose devices are as sharply defined as one could expect for on a business striking. The noticeably abraded, scuffy appearance accounts for the grade, but the thickly frosted devices, fully mirrored fields, and rich orange-rose patina provide relatively pleasing eye appeal. A moderate abrasion in the obverse field between stars 4 and 5 should be useful as a pedigree marker." A great rarity among Liberty double eagles with real potential to reach six figures. Population: 1 in 60, 2 finer (11/06).
From The Kutasi Collection.(#8996)

Challenging 1882-CC Double Eagle MS62

3205   1882-CC MS62 PCGS. Variety 2-B. Attributable by the first C in the mintmark being lower than the second. As often seen on this die pairing, a peripheral die crack nearly encircles the reverse. Although lightly circulated examples of the 1882-CC are not particularly difficult by Carson City twenty standards, attractive Mint State pieces are seldom offered (notwithstanding multiple offerings in this night's platinum session). Both sides of this satiny representative are boldly defined and only a few grade-limiting marks come into play on the obverse.
From The Kutasi Collection.(#8997)

Conditionally Scarce 1882-S
Double Eagle MS63

3206   1882-S MS63 PCGS. As is true with all of the S-mint double eagles from the 1880s, the 1882-S was struck in substantial numbers and can be found without too much difficulty in average Uncirculated grades. Mint State survivors are almost invariably very well struck and possess excellent luster characteristics. From the modern collector's perspective, problems arose with the way these coins were stored and transported. Heavy abrasions plague nearly all survivors to the extent that even a Select coin such as this is legitimately scarce. This example displays a vibrant, satiny appearance and is tinged in delicate orange patina. Population: 28 in 63, 1 finer (11/06).
From The Kutasi Collection.(#8998)

Sharp 1883-S Twenty, MS63 PCGS

3207   1883-S MS63 PCGS. Brass-gold color is visible in the centers of this Select double eagle, while a lime gold hue can be seen in the low points and peripheries. Well struck, as is usual for this date, which is generally considered obtainable only in grades up to MS62. The surfaces are fully lustrous and show a minimum of distracting marks. Population: 115 in 63, 8 finer (11/06).
From The Kutasi Collection.(#9000)

Beautiful Near-Gem 1884-S Double Eagle

3208   1884-S MS64 PCGS. Despite a plentiful mintage for the issue of 916,000 business strikes, like so many Type Three Liberty double eagles—especially S-mint issues—the 1884-S is common in lower grades up to and including MS62, but rare in MS63 and higher. Indeed, this is one of only 17 examples so graded at PCGS, with none finer (11/06). Regardless of the numerical grade, this piece is clearly head and shoulders above most survivors of this series, with its bold combination of sharp strike, pristine surfaces, potent luster, and beautiful apricot-gold center with greenish-gold at the borders. One hesitates to call attention to light abrasions that appear under a glass, as they are completely undistracting.
From The Kutasi Collection.(#9002)

Low-Mintage, Scarce MS61
1885-CC Twenty

3209   1885-CC MS61 PCGS. This low-mintage issue was man-ufactured only to the extent of 9,450 pieces, and accordingly ex-amples are scarce in all grades. Most of that mintage circulated extensively out West, but an occasional Mint State piece surfaces, such as this charming and attractive example. Deep greenish-gold coloration complements good luster, with a few grade-consistent abrasions noted under a glass. PCGS has graded nine pieces in MS61, with 10 coins finer, while NGC has certified three MS61 piec-es and three finer (11/06). A strong bid should take this lot.
From The Kutasi Collection.(#9004)

Sharp 1885-S Double Eagle MS64

3210   1885-S MS64 PCGS. Once the California gold rush began in earnest, it wasn't long before the bulk of double eagle production became the responsibility of the newly opened San Francisco Mint. By 1856 the mintage of S-mint twenties exceeded one million piec-es and output continued at a frantic pace throughout the Civil War. It is therefore extremely curious that no double eagles were struck in San Francisco in the year 1886. Offered here is a second Choice representative from the previous year. Like the coin just offered, this piece is well detailed and shows far fewer surface marks than is nor-mally encountered for the issue.
From The Kutasi Collection.(#9005)

Rare 1886 Double Eagle AU55

3211   1886 AU55 PCGS. Only 1,000 pieces were struck of the 1886 and it is even more difficult to locate in overall rarity than the 1881 and 1885. Some 25-30 pieces are believed extant today in all grades with perhaps only 7-9 coins known in the various grades of Almost Uncirculated. As with the 1885, and all 1886 twenties we have seen, the fields show considerable reflectivity. There is a significant overlay of reddish patina over each side. There are the small abrasions one would expect from a coin that has seen five points of wear, but the only ones of note are located in the field in front of Liberty's nose, out from star 13, and above the second T in TWENTY on the reverse. An exceptionally rare coin and possibly Condition Census quality. Population: 4 in 55, 5 finer (11/06).
From The Kutasi Collection.(#9006)

High Quality 1887-S Double Eagle

3212   1887-S MS63 PCGS. After a one-year hiatus in S-mint double eagle production, a comparatively modest mintage of 283,000 pieces was issued in 1887. These were the only business strike twenties coined this year at any of the four mints. As with other San Francisco issues from the decade, a fairly generous supply of Uncirculated coins is available for the 21st century collector. A normal propensity for abrasions keeps the vast majority of these well down the Mint State ladder. Field marks on this satiny, well defined example are generally light and unobtrusive. Only a hairline blemish above star 1 merits individual mention. Population: 45 in 63, 4 finer (11/06).
From The Kutasi Collection.(#9007)

Attractive MS62 1888 Double Eagle

3213   1888 MS62 PCGS. The 1888 is one of the few obtainable P-mint double eagles from the decade, yet becomes scarce once it exceeds the MS62 grade awarded to this coin, whose peach-gold fields surround frosty devices. Luster is attractive, particularly on the reverse. Surface abrasions, none worthy of singular mention, are in line with the grade.
From The Kutasi Collection.(#9008)

Conditionally Scarce 1888-S Twenty MS64

3214   1888-S MS64 PCGS. Well struck and highly lustrous, with lovely mint-green and rose-gold toning across each side. The reverse seems unusually clean, for a near-Gem. According to Garrett and Guth (2006): "There are no known specimens in gem condition. There have been several MS-64 coins offered at auction in 2005. Most have sold for around $10,000." Population: 39 in 64, 0 finer (11/06).
From The Kutasi Collection.(#9009)

Lustrous Mint State 1889 Double Eagle

3215   1889 MS62 PCGS. Boldly struck and highly lustrous with lovely lime-green and red-orange coloration. A mildly scuffy appearance on the obverse defines the numerical grade level of this attractive Mint State coin. Fewer than 45,000 business strike double eagles were produced in Philadelphia in 1889. As a result, it is a scarce issue in AU55 and finer grades, with none certified any higher than MS63 at either of the major services. Population: 81 in 62, 12 finer (11/06).
From The Kutasi Collection.(#9010)

Lustrous 1889-CC Double Eagle MS62

3216   1889-CC MS62 PCGS. While only a median rarity among Carson City double eagles, the supply of 1889-CC twenties begins to taper off rather quickly once the Mint State threshold is reached. Here survivors are generally clustered in the MS60 to MS62 grade range and are almost never seen finer. This example, while not quite reaching the Select category (although coming temptingly close), benefits from splendid golden-orange color and scintillating luster. Just a few too many shallow facial marks apparently preclude an MS63 rating. Population: 49 in 62, 6 finer (11/06).
From The Kutasi Collection.(#9011)

Scarce Select 1890 Double Eagle

3218   1890 MS63 PCGS. Orange and green-gold patina proclaims the originality of this lustrous and evenly struck double eagle. Moderately abraded, as usual for this low mintage date. Only 75,940 pieces were struck, a premonition of the ultra-rare 1891 and 1892 issues. Population: 36 in 63, 5 finer (11/06).
From The Kutasi Collection.(#9013)

Lustrous MS62 1890-CC Double Eagle

3219   1890-CC MS62 PCGS. The 1890-CC is the most available issue double eagle issue from the fabled Carson City mint, and is thus popular as a type coin. However, it is seldom found in grades finer than has been awarded to this attractive, lustrous, peach-orange coin, which features a good deal of mint frost on the devices in contrast with fields that hint at prooflikeness. A number of small abrasions define the grade but do not unduly affect the eye appeal. Population: 39 in 62, 7 finer (11/06).
From The Kutasi Collection.(#9014)

Rare Near-Gem 1889-S Double Eagle

3217   1889-S MS64 PCGS. This is an extremely important offering. Neither PCGS nor NGC have ever graded a finer example of the date, a true condition rarity. Over the years, we have only offered two previous examples of this date at the MS64 grade level. In *A Guide Book of Double Eagle Gold Coins,* Dave Bowers gave this date only a half page, stating simply: "The formula for San Francisco Mint double eagles of the 1880s holds true for this, the concluding year: examples are readily available in circulated grades and in Mint State from 60 to 62. Any higher grade coin is rare, curiously so." A sharply struck and highly lustrous near-Gem with frosty yellow-gold surfaces. Faint pinkish overtones are noted on each side, mostly hidden within the devices. Aside from the usual tiny chatter, the surfaces are free of any distracting marks. Population: 8 in 64, 0 finer (11/06).
From The Kutasi Collection.(#9012)

Sharp 1890-CC Double Eagle, MS62 PCGS

3220   1890-CC MS62 PCGS. A sharply struck example of this popular CC issue, bathed in radiant mint luster. The devices retain a good deal of mint frost, while the lime and peach-gold fields are more satiny in appearance. Traces of die doubling are visible over TWENTY and E PLURIBUS, as is often seen on the date. Rare in finer grades.
From The Kutasi Collection.(#9014)

Frosty Select 1890-S Double Eagle

3221   1890-S MS63 PCGS. Overpowering frosty luster is the first thing one notices when examining this coin, whose apricot-gold hues give way to a hint of lime-gold in the peripheries. Surface abrasions appear to define the grade, but do little to limit the eye appeal. Although not a difficult coin to find in an absolute sense, it is the rarest S-Mint issue of the 1890s and becomes scarce in grades higher than the current piece.

From The Kutasi Collection.(#9015)

Low Mintage 1891 Double Eagle
AU58 Prooflike

3222   1891 AU58 Prooflike NGC. Extensively abraded but seemingly free of highpoint wear, this flashy, near-Mint example more than compensates for its bagmarked appearance with dynamically reflective fields and surfaces that are awash in rich reddish-golden color and subtle lime-green undertones. The bold striking details, like the prooflike luster, are both characteristic of this elusive issue of just 1,390 business strikes. Across the country and at the other end of the spectrum, the San Francisco Mint cranked out nearly 1.3 million pieces this year. Within two short years the Philadelphia Mint would begin to more evenly share the burden of double eagle production.

According to Michael Fuljenz and Douglas Winter (2000): "The 1891 Double Eagle is very rare in all grades. It is generally found in Extremely Fine or in the lower ranges of About Uncirculated. It becomes very rare in the higher About Uncirculated grades and extremely rare in Mint State." We would add that a total of just five Uncirculated pieces, including the one with a prooflike designation, have been certified by both major services. It seems likely that at least one of these is a resubmission. Obviously, with the Prooflike designation as a part of its grade assessment, the issue is even more rare, as evidenced by the NGC Census report of: 1 in 58 Prooflike, 1 finer (11/06). *From The Kutasi Collection.*(#9016)

Frosty Choice 1891-S Twenty

3224 1891-S MS64 PCGS. Thick mint frost covers the surfaces of this double eagle, particularly on the reverse. The color of the obverse ranges from peach-gold to orange-gold, with a pinkish sheen over Liberty's features, while the reverse carries more of an olive-gold hue. The strike is exacting, and detail is full. Although this is a common date in low grades, it is scarce as fine as this piece's MS64, and only two have been certified MS65 at NGC (11/06).
From The Kutasi Collection.(#9018)

High End Near-Gem 1892-S Double Eagle

3225 1892-S MS64 PCGS. The obverse of this piece is surprisingly clean for the grade and, for accuracy alone, we report just a couple of extremely trivial field marks. The reverse displays even less evidence of coin-to-coin contact and/or improper handling. The surfaces exhibit attractive, swirling mint frost and crisply defined features. A scarce issue at this grade level, PCGS reports 69 examples certified at MS64, but none graded any finer (11/06).
From The Kutasi Collection.(#9021)

PCGS Choice 1893 Twenty, None Certified Finer

3226 1893 MS64 PCGS. Generally peach-gold in color, with lime-green visible in the peripheries and pink mint frost covering most of Liberty's features. Fully lustrous, with a few surface marks seemingly defining the grade. Virtually unobtainable finer, as the major services combined have seen fit to award Gem grades to only three coins of the date. Population: 59 in 64, 0 finer (11/06).
From The Kutasi Collection.(#9022)

Scarce 1891-CC Double Eagle MS61

3223 1891-CC MS61 PCGS. The 5,000 piece mintage of this issue is the second-lowest for a double eagle from the Carson City Mint. The '91-CC is surprisingly not rare in circulated grades, considering its skimpy mintage; but it is very scarce in Mint State, and the single highest-graded example is an MS63 at PCGS. This piece is highly lustrous, and cartwheel effects are easily noticeable on the obverse. The light lime-gold and peach toning is appealing. Definitely well struck, with all of the obverse stars and each of Liberty's hair strands crisply defined, which is unusual for any date in the series. A few spots and scattered, minuscule blemishes limit the grade. Population: 9 in 61, 5 finer (11/06).
From The Kutasi Collection.(#9017)

Scarce Select Mint State 1893-CC Twenty

3227   1893-CC MS63 PCGS. This Select quality double eagle is from the Carson City Mint's final issue. It seems very nice for the grade, and not "market-graded". The shimmering satiny luster and yellow-gold toning, with peach highlights, is very attractive. Most numismatists would rate this as a well struck piece, despite a hint of weakness on some the design's highest points. A faint smudge mark on the back of and just behind Liberty's hair bun is probably from a speck of grease on the die at the time of striking. "Choice examples are very scarce, and only one coin has been certified at the MS-64 level," according to Garrett and Guth's *Encyclopedia of U.S. Gold Coins.* Population: 18 in 63, 0 finer (11/06).
From The Kutasi Collection.(#9023)

Lovely Near-Gem 1893-S Double Eagle

3228   1893-S MS64 PCGS. Despite a mintage approaching one million coins, few survivors of this issue have such remarkable eye appeal and overall quality. This example is highly lustrous with brilliant yellow-gold color accented by wispy pink toning. The surfaces are satiny and delightful with no unsightly marks. All of the design elements on both sides are extremely sharp. Only the first two stars show any signs of weakness with all other details fully defined. This is only the second time we have offered a PCGS-certified example at this grade level since 1993. Population: 35 in 64, 1 finer (11/06).
From The Kutasi Collection.(#9024)

Choice BU 1894 Double Eagle

3229   1894 MS64 PCGS. Light apricot-gold over the upper obverse gives way to areas of orange- and lime- and olive-gold over the lower obverse and reverse. Satin luster pervades the surfaces, which are host to a minimum of intrusive marks. Exceptionally difficult to find nicer, with the major services combining to certify only six pieces in Gem and finer grades. Population: 87 in 64, 1 finer (11/06).
From The Kutasi Collection.(#9025)

Attractive Near-Gem 1894-S Twenty

3230   1894-S MS64 PCGS. This Choice piece is bright peach-gold with a small area of bronze-gold above the motto on the reverse. Strong satin luster covers the surfaces, which bear a few abrasions that seemingly account for the grade but do not harm the coin's appeal. Gems of this date are quite rare, and the discriminating date collector might do well to consider an attractive MS64 piece like this coin. Population: 114 in 64, 1 finer (11/06).
From The Kutasi Collection.(#9026)

Lustrous 1895 Double Eagle, MS64 PCGS

3231   1895 MS64 PCGS. This is a sharply detailed and highly lustrous piece, bathed in satin peach-gold color. Liberty's head shows a good deal of rose-gold mint frost. The few surface marks that exist do little to detract from this coin's formidable eye appeal. Exceptionally rare in finer grades, and likely headed to an outstanding date collection. Population: 175 in 64, 2 finer (11/06).
From The Kutasi Collection.(#9027)

Frosty 1895-S Twenty, MS64 PCGS

3232   1895-S MS64 PCGS. Heavy frosty luster covers this coin, whose gold color is interrupted only by a few surface grazes, which account for the grade. Blessed with a full strike, this is an appealing example of an otherwise common coin that is virtually unobtainable in Gem or finer condition. Population: 136 in 64, 6 finer (11/06).
From The Kutasi Collection.(#9028)

Fully Struck Choice 1896 Twenty

3233   1896 MS64 PCGS. Another example of a double eagle issue that is abundant in the lower Mint State grades, yet the supply of survivors drops precipitously at the near-Gem level. This is an especially attractive coin that is fully struck with pale lilac and orange-gold surfaces. PCGS has graded only two specimens, both MS65s, finer (11/06).
From The Kutasi Collection.(#9029)

Lustrous 1896-S Double Eagle, MS64 PCGS

3234 **1896-S MS64 PCGS.** The date collector searching for the finest possible 1896-S double eagle has three choices. He can wait, perhaps a generation, until the incredible MS67 Eliasberg coin becomes available. He can wait for the single NGC-graded MS65 specimen, bearing in mind that it too may not come up for sale for years and adding that even an image of the piece may be impossible to come by. Or he can choose to bid on a coin like the present piece, an appealing MS64 specimen with bright, mostly green-gold surfaces and complete luster. The strike is a bit weak on the upper obverse stars and the denomination, yet that is not uncommon with this date. Population: 129 in 64, 1 finer (11/06).
From The Kutasi Collection.(#9030)

Delightful 1897 Double Eagle, MS64 PCGS

3235 **1897 MS64 PCGS.** Thick satin luster envelops the surfaces of this attractive apricot-gold coin. Surface markings are curiously unobtrusive for the grade. A series of tiny die cracks (as struck) is visible through the left obverse periphery and date. Only twelve pieces of this date have been certified finer, and it is open to question whether they can match this coin for eye appeal. Population: 141 in 64, 1 finer (11/06).
From The Kutasi Collection.(#9031)

Satiny Choice 1897-S Twenty

3236 **1897-S MS64 PCGS.** Peach-gold hues intermix with splash of olive and lime-green over this satiny Choice double eagle. A few light marks, in line with the grade, dot the coin's surfaces, yet do not interfere with the full luster. Exceptionally difficult to find nicer. Population: 248 in 64, 4 finer (11/06).
From The Kutasi Collection.(#9032)

Elusive Select Mint State 1898 Twenty

3237 **1898 MS63 PCGS.** Bright and satiny, with fine grain, matte-like surfaces and alluring peach, rose, and green-gold coloration. A few wispy marks are noticeable on the obverse, but the reverse is remarkably clean for the grade. According to Q. David Bowers (2004): "Today the 1898 in Mint State is usually seen in MS-60 to MS-62, much less often in MS-63, and hardly ever finer." As a matter of fact, PCGS has only graded seven pieces higher, all of them at MS64 (11/06).
From The Kutasi Collection.(#9033)

Scarce Gem 1898-S Liberty Head Twenty

3238 **1898-S MS65 PCGS.** The subtly variegated lime-green and peach tinting is well illuminated by flashy cartwheel luster on both sides. The striking details are impeccable, and even the often-suspect obverse hair and reverse eagle elements are crisply delineated. Only superficial marks are noticed, on Liberty's cheek and in the left obverse field. PCGS has graded just two pieces finer (11/06).
From The Kutasi Collection.(#9034)

Elusive Choice Uncirculated 1899-S Twenty

3240   1899-S MS64 PCGS. Very common in grades ranging from XF to MS63, this issue becomes scarce at the Choice Uncirculated level, and rare any finer. This near-Gem is well struck and boasts dynamic luster, along with eye-pleasing lime-gold and rose patina. Minor marks on Liberty's cheek and in the left obverse field prevent a higher grade.
From The Kutasi Collection.(#9036)

Lovely Turn-of-The-Century Gem Double Eagle

3241   1900 MS65 PCGS. The eye of the viewer is immediately drawn to the splendid, subtly variegated toning scheme, that includes lime-green and peach as two of its primary colors. The distinctly matte-like surfaces are bright and highly lustrous. A strong striking impression is implied by the uniformly crisp design details, and minimal marks are found on either side. A lovely, beautifully preserved Gem. Population: 50 in 65, 2 finer (11/06).
From The Kutasi Collection.(#9037)

Highly Desirable Gem 1899 Double Eagle

3239   1899 MS65 PCGS. Lovely peach-gold, rose, and mint-green toning adorns the flashy surfaces of this well preserved Gem. Ebullient cartwheel luster shimmers through the fields on both obverse and reverse. As befits the issue, the design features display razor-sharp delineation that leaves no element weakly defined. The 1899 double eagle is a very common coin in lower Mint State grades, through MS63. The numbers fall off considerably between MS63 and MS64, however. At the Gem preservation level this date suddenly becomes very scarce, especially at PCGS where just eight pieces have been so graded, and none finer (11/06). One thing about this example seems clear: when it crosses the auction block, double eagle specialists are certain to sit up and take notice.
From The Kutasi Collection.(#9035)

Extremely Scarce Gem 1900-S Double Eagle

3242   1900-S MS65 PCGS. The intense luster that rolls across each side of this visually alluring Gem is perhaps its most noteworthy attribute; but the lovely yellow-gold and mint-green coloration is not far behind. Both of these features combine together to ensure the strong overall eye appeal of the piece. The meticulously struck design elements are uniform on both sides, except only for obverse stars 1 and 2 and a few of the denticles. A minor scuff mark on Liberty's cheek is unfortunate, but does little to impair the overall visual quality of the coin. The fields on each side are remarkably clean for one of these large, heavy gold coins. Somewhat common in lower grades, this issue is exceedingly scarce at the Gem level of preservation, with fewer than 10 pieces so graded at NGC and PCGS combined. PCGS Population: 3 in 65, 0 finer (11/06).
From The Kutasi Collection.(#9038)

High Quality Gem 1901 Double Eagle

3243   1901 MS65 PCGS. Garrett and Guth (2006) report that a large hoard of high quality examples of this date emerged during the 1990s, making the 1901 a popular issue for type purposes. This example is fully struck and displays intense, vibrant luster. The variegated toning scheme is highly attractive. A few scattered marks are noted, but the overall quality of the piece pronounces it a Gem. Encapsulated in a green label holder.
From The Kutasi Collection.(#9039)

Conditionally Scarce 1901-S Twenty MS64

3244   1901-S MS64 PCGS. A crisply struck and carefully preserved green-gold representative. Courtesy of a generous production, the 1901-S is plentiful in typical Mint State grades. But since these piece were indifferently stored, few have maintained relatively unblemished surfaces. Population: 81 in 64, 2 finer (11/06).
From The Kutasi Collection.(#9040)

Select Mint State 1902 Double Eagle

3245   1902 MS63 PCGS. This low mintage issue is scarce at all grade levels, very challenging in Select Mint State, and rare any finer. The essentially full striking details exhibited by the current example are its most noteworthy feature. It is also nicely preserved and highly lustrous, with bright lime-gold toning. A significant opportunity for the specialist in Liberty Head double eagles. Population: 59 in 63, 8 finer (11/06).
From The Kutasi Collection.(#9041)

Attractive 1902-S Double Eagle MS63 PCGS

3246   1902-S MS63 PCGS. Essentially well struck, although the eagle's right (facing) talon is softly defined. Bright satiny luster and lovely, light peach and mint-green toning enhance the eye appeal of the piece. Moderate marks are noted near obverse star 5 and Liberty's eye, along with scattered minor blemishes on both sides. *From The Kutasi Collection.*(#9042)

Flashy Gem 1903 Double Eagle

3247   1903 MS65 PCGS. All of the design elements are sharply detailed, even those that often show weakness. Flashy, coruscant mint frost shimmers over both sides of this pleasing Gem. The mixture of mint-green and honey-gold toning is highly attractive. Modest marks on the obverse preclude an even finer grade assessment. PCGS has certified just two finer examples of this issue (11/06). *From The Kutasi Collection.*(#9043)

Radiant Gem 1903-S Double Eagle

3248   1903-S MS65 PCGS. An uncommonly smooth representative of this otherwise readily obtainable S-mint double eagle, the richly frosted surfaces possess lovely cartwheel visual effects and are accented with delicate reddish-orange patina. Sharply struck with largely undisturbed fields and just a few wispy abrasions on Liberty's cheek and brow. One of just five different Gem 1903-S twenties (several were repeated) we have offered over the past decade, the most recent being sold last September for nearly $11,000. Population: 7 in 65, 0 finer (11/06). *From The Kutasi Collection.*(#9044)

Premium Gem 1904 Double Eagle

3249   1904 MS66 PCGS. Among the many thousands of Uncirculated survivors of this most available Liberty double eagle, the natural tendency for these soft, heavy gold coins to pick up a few abrasions along the way is almost inescapable. Endowed with a strong strike and vibrant, satiny luster, this lovely Premium Gem is even more remarkable in its lack of surface marks. Of equal importance, the sole mentionable disturbance is an out-of-the-way milling mark hidden in Liberty's hair. Had this mark been placed smack dab in the middle of Liberty's cheek, the numeric grade would have surely been penalized. An outstanding, nearly unsurpassable type coin.
From The Kutasi Collection.(#9045)

Lustrous Gem 1904-S Twenty Dollar

3250   1904-S MS65 PCGS. Well struck with shimmering mint luster and pleasing green-gold and rose patina. A few stray marks are seen on each side, but they seem consistent with the Gem grade assessment. A small charcoal-colored speck is noted near the left edge of the 1 in the date, but has little effect on the coin's pleasing overall appearance. Essentially unobtainable any finer, with just two MS66s known, one from each of the two major services (11/06).
From The Kutasi Collection.(#9046)

Low Mintage 1905 Double Eagle MS63

3251   1905 MS63 PCGS. Following a mammoth production of more than six million pieces in 1904, the Philadelphia Mint took a little breather from the minting of double eagles the following year when output plummeted to just 58,900 coins. It appears that most of this small output found its way into the channels of commerce, as only a few hundred Mint State pieces are extant. Factor in a propensity for heavy abrasions and even Select examples such as this are quite scarce. Offered here is a satiny, moderately abraded representative with no individually distracting marks. The location of a finer specimen would not only be extremely challenging, but at least double the cost.

From The Kutasi Collection.(#9047)

Attractive Choice 1905-S Double Eagle

3252   1905-S MS64 PCGS. Although available in lower Mint State grades, the 1905-S is considered a better date once it reaches the Select level of preservation. This piece is nicer still, of course, and indeed appears to be blessed with a lower than average number of surface abrasions for the grade. Peach-gold in color, the coin possesses an attractive satiny luster and shows just the merest hint of a mirrored surface on the reverse. Population: 125 in 64, 7 finer (11/06).

From The Kutasi Collection.(#9048)

Conditionally Scarce Gem 1906 Twenty

3253   1906 MS65 PCGS. The overall quality of this conditionally scarce Gem is quite astonishing. The rich mint frost over both sides creates a beautiful sheen that highlights the powerfully struck devices and the amazingly clean fields. The lovely honey-gold coloration is imbued with occasional accents of light orange. Faint chatter on the cheek, and a minor graze in the obverse field, just to the left of Liberty's nose, are the only slight flaws to be found on this highly desirable example. The combined populations of NGC and PCGS show 11 coins certified at MS65, and two graded MS66 (11/06).
From The Kutasi Collection.(#9049)

Elusive Gem 1906-D Double Eagle

3254   1906-D MS65 PCGS. After serving as a United States Assay Office for more than 40 years, the Denver Mint commenced operations in 1906 and made an immediate impact in the production of both silver and gold coinage. The new facility struck more than half of the gold eagles produced this year and contributed over 20 percent of the gold double eagle production. Perhaps due in part to its first year status, thousands of Uncirculated twenties were saved for posterity and survivors through the MS63 grade tier are easily acquired. There is a noticeable drop-off at the Choice level and Gems such as this piece are actually quite scarce. The satiny surfaces exhibit a uniform reddish-golden tint and are remarkable void of abrasions. Population: 4 in 65, 0 finer (11/06).
From The Kutasi Collection.(#9050)

Choice Mint State 1906-S Double Eagle

3255   1906-S MS64 PCGS. San Franciscans to this day recall 1906 as the year of the great earthquake and fire. The mint at Fifth and Mission Streets, the "Granite Lady," was virtually the only structure that survived the disaster intact, and it served multiple duties in those days as a headquarters for relief and rescue efforts and as a coiner of money. One can only speculate whether this piece, born in San Francisco during the same year, bore witness to the quake, but if it did, it emerged virtually unscathed, as over 100 years later it retains full luster over its soft, attractive, peach-gold surfaces. Numismatists are often interested in coins that recall both a particular time and place. Those with a connection to Northern California might just find this piece to their liking. Population: 192 in 64, 3 finer (11/06).

From The Kutasi Collection.(#9051)

Gem 1907-S Twenty, Finest-Graded at PCGS

3257   1907-S MS65 PCGS. Despite a high mintage of 2,165,800 pieces, the '07-S is not a common coin. An extremely important opportunity is presented here, for this is the only example of the issue to be certified as a Gem by PCGS. From an aesthetic perspective, we cannot imagine what a finer example would look like. Both sides have frosty and attractively toned surfaces, with variegated red-orange and greenish-gray color. All of the design elements are sharply defined. This was the final Liberty Head double eagle issue from the San Francisco Mint. Population: 1 in 65, 0 finer (11/06).

From The Kutasi Collection.(#9054)

3256   1907-D MS65 PCGS. This amazingly clean Gem displays a full strike and frosty, radiantly lustrous surfaces on obverse and reverse alike. The subtle color variations include peach, reddish-gold, and pastel-green. While the reverse seems pristine, the obverse has a few very superficial marks at the lower portion. One of only two Denver Mint Liberty double eagles and always a popular issue. Scarce in finer grades.

From The Kutasi Collection.(#9053)

Amazing Gem 1907-D Twenty

ULTRA HIGH RELIEF DOUBLE EAGLE, PR68 PCGS

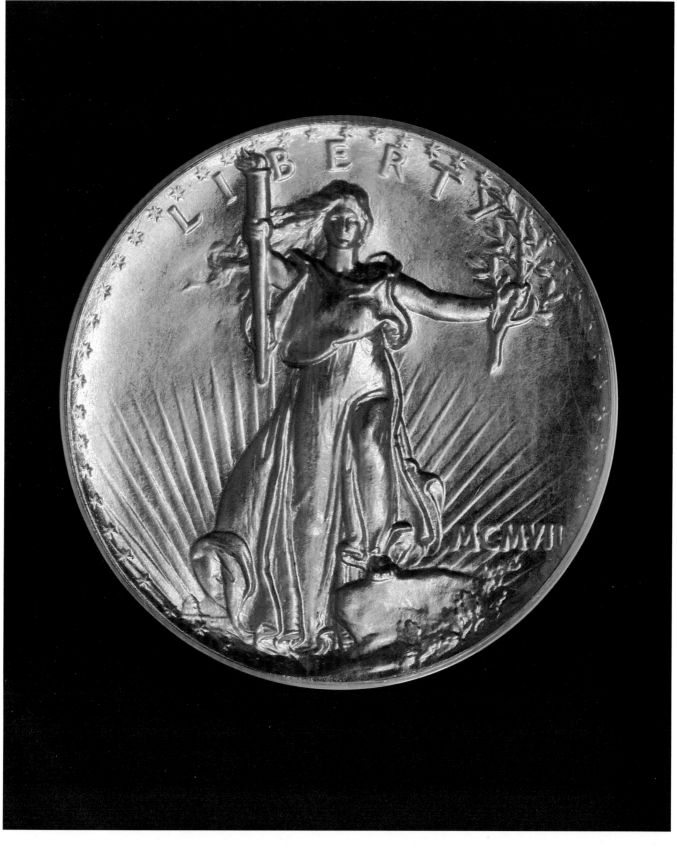

Extraordinary 1907 Ultra High Relief Double Eagle, PR68 PCGS

3258   1907 Ultra High Relief Lettered Edge PR68 PCGS. Among American coin collectors, the Saint-Gaudens Ultra (or Extremely) High Relief double eagle coin may be the most recognized coin ever produced. There are other great rarities of outstanding reputation, but no other combines the beauty, rarity, and the story of collaboration between President Theodore Roosevelt and Augustus Saint-Gaudens.

Theodore Roosevelt became President after the assassination of William McKinley in September 1901. After three years of being President one would think he had adapted to the job, yet it was not until after the election of November 1904 that Roosevelt could truly claim in his own thoughts to be President of the United States.

In the weeks following his election, amid celebrations and congratulatory visits, there was time for contemplation and good-natured conversation with wife Edith, and family friend, painter Frank Millet. As their conversations wandered over many topics, the subject of the aesthetic merit of American coinage came to the fore. It probably took little prodding for Millet to expound on the artistic banalities of the coins Americans carried in their pockets and purses. Roosevelt agreed and soon fired off a typically commanding letter to Secretary of the Treasury Leslie Mortier Shaw on December 27, 1904:

My dear Secretary Shaw:
I think our coinage is artistically of atrocious hideousness. Would it be possible, without asking permission of Congress, to employ a man like Saint-Gaudens to give us a coinage that would have some beauty?

The President had developed an opinion and now wanted to do something about it—he was not one to study the situation at length. With Shaw's assurance that Saint-Gaudens could be hired to design American coins, Roosevelt laid his trap. For his part, by 1905 Saint-Gaudens was at the height of reputation in America and Europe. As early as 1887, he had turned down suggestions that he redesign the nation's coinage. Since an 1894 disagreement over the Columbia Exposition medal with the Mint Bureau, he had wanted nothing to do with work for the U.S. Government.

The artist and politician had been acquainted at least since the 1890s when they both attended evening discussions at Henry James' home in New York. Since Roosevelt's election as Vice President, he had consistently praised the artist in letters and public comments, but now, with a purpose in mind, intense ego-stroking began. First came a lavish banquet at the American Institute of Architects (AIA) on January 11, 1905 with Saint-Gaudens and Roosevelt both attending. This was followed by the annual Diplomatic Reception at the White House on January 12. After the reception, Saint-Gaudens was ushered upstairs for dinner amid the glow of candles, gold-and-velvet uniforms and waves of ladies in shimmering silk. Saint-Gaudens was seated next to Edith Roosevelt, well above many representatives of other nations. During these events, Roosevelt evidently outlined his grand plan to remake the coinage. Like any good sportsman, the President set fresh bait for his quarry: first design an Inaugural Medal.

Less than three weeks after the letter to Shaw, Roosevelt had button-holed Saint-Gaudens and flattered, cajoled, and possibly bullied the artist into accepting the task of designing the medal and redesigning the coinage. The medal was completed (with much assistance from Adolph Weinman) within a few months. But it would be two long years before the first experimental coins were struck. During that time, and through the few months of life that remained for Saint-Gaudens, the artist and politician would never meet again.

It was the summer of 1905 before Saint-Gaudens formally accepted the President's coinage design commission. For the sum of $5,000 the sculptor was to produce one pair of obverse and reverse designs for use on all four circulating gold coins, and another pair of different designs for the bronze cent. These were the only coins eligible for change under the Coinage Act of 1890. Over the next 18 months the President and sculptor exchanged letters filled with suggestions and supportive comments. First priority went to the large gold coins, impressive and most appealing to Roosevelt. The practicalities of production were never mentioned except when Mint Director George Roberts or Secretary Shaw were consulted. By the beginning of June 1906, Saint-Gaudens had prepared his designs and shipped off the plaster reverse model, showing a standing eagle based on his 1905 Roosevelt Inaugural medal, to Paris for reductions. The completed work returned in the Fall and everything should have been ready to turn over to the Philadelphia Mint. But, the sculptor sensed something was not right about his designs.

Through late September, October, November, and into December, Saint-Gaudens struggled to rework his creations. Meanwhile, Roosevelt was getting anxious to have final models and wrote to the artist on December 11:

I hate to trouble you, but it is very important that I should have the models for those coins at once. How soon may I have them?
With all good wishes, believe me,

Saint-Gaudens responded by sending models to the White House on December 14. However, they were not the ones President Roosevelt had expected. The only obverse and reverse designs anyone with the administration had seen were of a Striding Liberty with wings and Indian headdress, and a standing eagle derived from the inaugural medal. The new models were simpler, stronger, the reverse now featured a flying eagle. During October and November, Saint-Gaudens had apparently been experimenting with his Striding Liberty without the wings and Indian headdress. He also replaced the original reverse with the now-familiar flying eagle. In a follow-up letter the artist apologized for markings that suggested these initial models were not finished:

I am afraid from the letter sent you on the fourteenth with the models for the Twenty Dollar Gold piece that you will think the coin I sent you was unfinished. This is not the case. It is the final and completed model, but I hold myself in readiness to make any such modifications as may be required in the reproduction of the coin.

This will explain the words "test model" on the back of each model.

When Roosevelt finally saw the large design models on December 15 he was hardly able to control his enthusiasm:

My dear Saint Gaudens:

Those models are simply immense—if such a slang way of talking is permissible in reference to giving a modern nation one coinage at least which shall be as good as that of the ancient Greeks. I have instructed the Director of the Mint that these dies are to be reproduced just as quickly as possible and just as they are. It is simply splendid. I suppose I shall be impeached for it in Congress; but I shall regard that as a very cheap payment!

With heartiest regards,

The President also reminded Mint Director Roberts of his expectations:

... I do want to ask that you have special and particular care exercised in the cutting of that Saint Gaudens coin. Won't you bring the die in for me to see, even before you send it to Saint Gaudens? Of course the workmanship counts as much as the design in a case like this. I feel that we have the chance with this coin to make something as beautiful as the old Greek coinage. In confidence, I am not at all sure how long I shall be permitted to have such a coin in existence; but I want for once at least to have had this nation, the great republic of the West ... do something in the way of artistic expression that shall rank with the best work of the kind that has ever been done.

Sincerely yours,

P.S. Of course keep what we are doing absolutely confidential, as I do not want anything about it to get out until the coins are actually made.

Roberts replied to the President the next day, including assurances that the Mint Bureau would do its best:

... I fully appreciate your interest in the Saint Gaudens designs, and join you in it. I shall be happy to have my administration of the mint service distinguished by the execution of this beautiful piece. I delivered the models myself to the Engraver at Philadelphia last week, and I am assured that every man in the mint who has to do with this work will do his utmost to make the coinage a success.

... I have no misgivings however about the execution of the dies; I believe that dies-cutting done at the mint is equal to any done in this country. But the high relief will present difficulties in coinage which have never yet been overcome, and when it comes to that we must ask your patience while we try to work out the problem ... The very best that can be done will be done to give effect to these designs.

I have cautioned everybody who of necessity must know of this undertaking that it is a confidential matter ...

"That is first-class. I am very much obliged to you," replied the President.

The models also omitted the motto E PLURIBUS UNUM and included no suggestions for the edge of the coin. Charles Barber commented about the edge motto and stars:

... Regarding the lettering upon the edge, if Mr. Saint Gaudens will send a sketch of the character of the letter he desires and also a sketch of the star to be used I will attend to the rest, which you know is made in the collar.

... Mr. Saint Gaudens need not go further than to furnish the sketches asked for with any instructions he wishes regarding the position of the letters and stars, whether they are to entirely encircle the coin or only partly, any of the directions given will be strictly adhered to.

It appears that Charles Barber created a lettered edge for Saint-Gaudens' design based on his experimental work in 1885 and a 1906 "proof of concept" sample assembled by he and assistant engraver George Morgan. This "proof of concept" coin was the Barber/Morgan twenty dollar pattern of 1906. This pattern was most likely made in late December 1906 to prove to Director Roberts that a raised lettered edge coin could be made without unusual difficulty.

As 1906 closed, President Theodore Roosevelt was at the peak of his popularity. The Nobel Peace Prize, awarded for negotiating an end to the Russo-Japanese War, had elevated him, and the country, from blustering backwater to an international force in the community of nations. This had boosted his popularity with the public, and muffled critics in the opposition and his own Republican Party.

Charles Edward Barber, Engraver of the United States Mint at Philadelphia, was pleased to have the new models in his workshop. Long ago he had decided no model from Saint-Gaudens' hand could be coined, but many artists were skeptical. Now he had what he needed to prove "the Saint" knew nothing of coinage. He was determined to do all he could to make coins out of the medallic designs Saint-Gaudens provided. With the information from this experiment at hand, he could finally put the sculptor in his place. He was also determined to make sure his superiors in the Bureau of the Mint knew it.

Anticipating a future assertion from Saint-Gaudens that the mint's dies or hubs were inferior, Barber turned to Henri Weil, a Paris-trained expert in the use of the Janvier reducing lathe, for assistance. Unknown to anyone except Director Roberts and the Philadelphia Mint Superintendent, Barber arranged for Henri Weil, a Dietsch Brothers employee, to help him make the reductions and hubs. Although the work was being done at the mint, bringing in an outside expert to cut the new hubs might not agree with Roosevelt. Confidentiality was important—no one wanted the President galloping through the Philadelphia Mint issuing orders.

Weil visited from January 3 through 8 and was officially explained as providing additional training on the new equipment. But what Weil did was to make paraffin reductions from the Saint-Gaudens' models, bronze casts of the reductions, and cut the high relief hubs. All this took six days during which Barber made notes so he could complete additional hubs on his own.

Apparently no attempt was made to lower the relief, this being Barber's understanding of the President's command to use the models "just as they are," so the full design was reduced proportionally. This process was much like what Barber had learned to do on the old Hill lathe 30 years earlier. The part the engravers did not learn was how to reduce relief while maintaining detail in all parts of the design. This knowledge gap would haunt the mint's work until John Sinnock became engraver in 1925.

With hubs cut by an expert known to Saint-Gaudens, Barber's experiment was to try and strike a coin from the new dies—something he knew would fail. The real problem was not high relief of the models, the Philadelphia Mint has been making high relief medals for a century, it was making detailed reductions (including relief) from large diameter models. A secondary problem was identifying how much relief was possible on a coin struck with just one blow of the production press. Working dies of the first models were completed within a month, and on February 15, 1907 the first gold impressions of the new double eagle were placed in the hands of the Director of the Mint. Roberts reimbursed the mint account for his coins and took them back to Washington.

This first small group of Extremely High Relief twenty dollar coins included three complete strikes, a plain edge (incompletely struck), and three partially struck pieces, all in gold. The complete coins had lettered edges using the segmented collar on the late 1906 experimental example. The plain edge, which was also the last one struck of this group, had a prominent die crack on the reverse. The intention was to strike a small quantity, possibly 15, but this was thwarted when the reverse die cracked.

The Assay Commission was meeting at the Philadelphia Mint at this time and it is likely that Dr. George Kunz and possibly others on the Assay Commission saw or were told about the new coins. On February 18 Kunz was advised, "Please say nothing at Numismatic Society or elsewhere about our new coins." Victor Brenner also learned about the new coins and was told, " ... it is not possible at present to give out information about the talked-of new coins."

Each complete experimental Extremely High Relief coin required seven blows at 150 tons pressure from the hydraulic press—six in a plain edge collar to bring up the design and a seventh in a three-part collar to impart edge lettering. Between each strike, the planchet was annealed to compensate for work hardening produced in the press. After heating to a deep red, the planchet was dipped into a weak nitric acid solution, which removed any oxidized copper from the surface. Repetition of this treatment left the coin's surface depleted of copper. All known Mint State specimens have the color of nearly pure gold rather than .900 fine alloy color.

Saint-Gaudens wrote to the Director on February 21 asking for casts of the coins and to examine the gold experimental pieces:

I find that if the Twenty Dollar gold coin required seven strikes, it will be necessary ... to have a cast of each of the following strikes sent me:
The First.
The Second.
The Fifth.
The Seventh.
The finished strike in lead.
The finished strike in lead of the small coin.
... It is also absolutely essential that I should also have the actual gold strikings described above, as it would give me a much truer idea of the result. I can assure you that I would take the best possible care of these strikings and return them to you in a very short time.

Director Roberts agreed to Saint-Gaudens' request, but learned that the mint could not supply everything requested:

The dies being broken I can only furnish such pieces as I have of the Double Eagle in gold, new design, namely; first, second, third strike and a finished piece, and one impression of each diameter, in lead, without the lettering on the periphery [i.e., edge].
I have no doubt that these will answer the desired purpose.
The finished coin is the best impression of the steel hub that can be furnished.

The gold coin and strike samples were duly sent to Saint-Gaudens and returned by him on March 13. The three complete coins from this first group use the same lettered edge with a plain sans-serif style font, and each letter in the motto was separated by a star.

The experimental coins received by Director Roberts had caused something of a stir at mint headquarters, and on March 4 Roberts authorized the production of two more samples specifically for the Philadelphia Mint cabinet of coins. To make more experimental pieces for the mint cabinet, Barber had to make a new working die from the hub. This was not completed until at least late March.

This second group of EHR coins had a new edge design that used a Roman (serif) font. The letters were upside down if the coin was viewed with the obverse facing up (called Alignment B-II). Although using this alignment for most of the EHR experimental coins might seem odd, it has a subtle elegance. If one looks at the obverse of the coin, then moves slightly to one side or the other, the edge lettering appears to be an extension of the coin's face, arching over the figure of Liberty, with the text reading correctly. This counter-intuitive approach enhances the three-dimensional effect of the design, and was certainly Saint-Gaudens' intent.

A third and final group of three coins were struck on New Years' Eve by Charles Barber at the request of Mint Director

Leach.

A total of three groups of Extremely High Relief pattern coins were struck at the Philadelphia Mint. The groups differ in the treatment of the edge. The estimated mintages are:

Group I—February 1907—Three complete coins, one plain edge coin.
Group II—March/April 1907—Thirteen (estimated) complete coins.
Group III—December 31, 1907—Three complete coins.

The total mintage is unknown. A reasonable estimate is that 18 to 20 pieces were struck, including the lone plain edge coin. The present specimen appears to be one of the Group II pieces, although the encapsulation prevents examination of the edge.

The magnificent Extremely High Relief patterns led to changes in design details, which finally resulted in the High Relief and Low Relief versions released into circulation late in 1907. The original hubs and dies were destroyed on May 24-25, 1910.

Diagnostics:

Working obverse and reverse dies for all versions of the EHR double eagles were made from the same hubs cut by Barber and Weil in January 1907. When compared to later versions, the EHR design has a very small Capitol building to Liberty's lower right (left as one views the coin), and the berries on the olive branch are few and indistinct. One star sits above each of the arms of the Y in LIBERTY.

The surfaces of this incredible coin are bright orange-gold. As mentioned above, this finish is the product of repeated annealings, which resulted in the eventual elimination of all copper from the alloy and a thin layer of pure gold over both obverse and reverse. The striking details are nothing short of extraordinary also with an even more pronounced, dished, three-dimensional effect than seen on a regular High Relief. After several minutes of examining this piece with a strong magnifier we finally were able to locate one surface flaw that might be used as a pedigree identifier for this important coin: There is a short, diagonal luster graze on the reverse between the eagle's head and the forward curve of the wing.

The opportunity to personally examine an Ultra High Relief is rare in itself. The opportunity to actually own one of these magnificent coins is a thrill few people will ever experience in their lifetime. For those who can seriously contemplate the purchase of such a coin, the offering of this piece at public auction is an event worthy of focused attention.
We are deeply indebted to numismatic researcher Roger Burdette for the above background information for the Extremely High Relief. All the information in this description is taken from primary sources.(#9131)

Augustus Saint-Gaudens

HIGH RELIEF DOUBLE EAGLE

Gem Flat Rim MCMVII High Relief

3259   1907 High Relief, Flat Rim MS65 PCGS. The thin golden fin (or "wire rim") commonly seen on earlier high relief double eagles was considered nothing less than a major defect by the mint. The fin was easily abraded and this had the potential for reducing the coin's weight to below legal standard. It was also an aesthetic problem that marred the otherwise magnificent and difficult to produce coins.

Using suggestions made by Director Leach (based on his years of working with gold at San Francisco), the Philadelphia Mint changed the way they milled the coin blanks. These alterations allowed coins to be struck with almost no fin and met with full approval from Roosevelt, "The President was greatly pleased with the sample of the lot now being struck off on the Medal press." Although the coins were noticeably superior to earlier pieces, engraver Charles Barber was concerned: "All the coins now made are the same, which gives me alarm, as they are so well made that I fear the President may demand the continuance of this particular coin."

Ultimately, cost and low productivity prevented more extensive coining of the high relief version. According to Roger Burdette, approximately one-third of the 12,367 pieces struck were of the finless variety. As with other High Relief twenties, they were shipped to sub-Treasuries in small bags that contained 250 pieces with little done to prevent nicks and scrapes. Only 58 High Relief coins were included with the Treasurer's little hoard of gold in 1912. All had been sold by February 1913 for an average of just $23.00 each.

Of all the variations on the initial double eagle design presented to the President in December 1906, the High Relief, Flat Rim coins are closest to a golden realization of Saint-Gaudens final design. Detail, execution and overall appearance are closest to the sculptor's last Very High Relief models of March 1907. Although the much-exalted Extremely High Relief experimental pieces get more publicity, it is this—an almost accidental coin—that truly embodies the artistic collaboration of Theodore Roosevelt and Augustus Saint-Gaudens.

This is a magnificent, Gem example of the Flat Rim variant. The surfaces have thick, satiny mint luster and are sharply defined, as one would expect from a coin that was struck three times with a hydraulic press. The MS65 grade, of course, precludes any noticeable or mentionable contact marks. Simply magnificent quality.
From The Kutasi Collection.(#9136)

Stunning MS67 1907 Low Relief Saint-Gaudens Twenty

3260   1907 Arabic Numerals MS67 PCGS. By June 20, 1907, Saint-Gaudens and Roosevelt had agreed that the double eagle should be struck in low relief and with the date in European digits. The sculptor's assistant, Henry Hering, was supposed to begin work on low relief models right away, but when Roosevelt decided to have a separate design for the ten dollar coin, everything was put aside so that new models could be prepared. The result was that nothing was done about the double eagle until after Saint-Gaudens died. By mid-August, with the president fuming at further delay, and no low relief twenty dollar models ready, Hering at last began the work. His sculpting went quickly and by September 20 he had completed the third and last set of double eagle models. These were sent to Philadelphia where reductions and hubbing were begun immediately. Had these low relief models been delivered in a timely manner, it is possible the entire 1907 issue of double eagles would have come from these models. It is also possible that there would have been no High Relief coins with Roman numeral date.

Barber made working dies and struck a few samples, but quickly realized that much of the fine detail had been lost in the process. Hering was called to the mint and the problem was discussed at length, but resulted in Hering doing nothing. With President Roosevelt demanding gold for circulation use, Director Leach and Charles Barber agreed to alter the hubs that had already been made. Much of his work consisted of re-engraving details lost during reduction of the final models. Using the High Relief version as a guide and his own judgment as to line depth, Barber succeeded in making changes in a manner that has proven elusive until the present. According to recent research by Roger Burdette, we now know that circulation dies came from Hering's plaster model, with European date, after Barber retouched the original hub. Thus, it is now known that the High Relief and Low Relief coins originated with different design models.

Imparting edge lettering under volume production conditions took considerable experimentation. The first 8,000 Low Relief twenties had to be destroyed, and it was not until December 6 that 15,000 acceptable pieces were struck. The new Low Relief coins were officially released on December 13. The coiner reported striking 361,667 new double eagles through the end of 1907.

Superb examples are rarely seen of the 1907 Low Relief. The present example is among the finest certified by both PCGS and NGC. Only five other PCGS coins have been certified in MS67 and eight have been so graded by NGC, with none finer at either service (10/06). The frosted surfaces show a light overlay of reddish patina with a fine granularity around the margins from slight metal flow. Fully struck throughout, with complete definition on the pillars of the Capitol building, there are no mentionable or noticeable marks on either side of this magnificent first-year issue.

From The Kutasi Collection.(#9141)

Superb MS67 Wells Fargo Twenty Dollar

3261   1908 No Motto, Wells Fargo Nevada MS67 PCGS. The November 3, 1997, edition of *Coin World* reported the acquisition of "a hoard of more than 15,000 coins ... earlier in 1997 for more than $10 million. Some 7,000 to 8,000 1908 Saint-Gaudens, No Motto double eagles graded MS-66 and lower are already in the hands of retail investors and collectors ... The No Motto double eagles were originally acquired around 1917 and they remained untouched until the early 1970s when they were sorted, counted and resealed in bags. The coins again remained untouched until they were moved about 1996." This spectacular hoard is the single source for high grade No Motto twenties for the gold type collector. This is a wonderfully clean example that has rich, swirling mint frost on each side. The striking details are sharply defined throughout, including the pillars on the Capitol building. Each side also displays a light, even overlay of reddish patina.
From The Kutasi Collection.(#99142)

Among the Finest Known 1908-D No Motto Twenties, MS66 PCGS

3262   1908-D No Motto MS66 PCGS. Long Rays. Orders were issued on February 4 to ship double eagle dies and edge collars to the Denver Mint. Along with the package came a message from engraver Charles Barber warning that the new coins would " ... not pile to standard height ..." This was a potentially serious problem because banks and counting houses (even the mint's own adjustors and coin counters) made trial balances using coins piled to the same height. If a stack were too short, a coin was added on the assumption that twenty pieces always made the same height stack. Twenty of the old Liberty Head twenty dollar gold pieces made a pile 1.937 inches high, but the new coins amounted only to 1.852 inches for twenty pieces—a difference of almost one full coin in height. By making new hubs, changing the width of the rim, and making the dies more convex, the mint was able to make the coins thicker and had solved this problem by the end of March.

The first Denver Mint coins also apparently shared the excess diameter problem with Philadelphia, but corrections were made, and coins issued after about March 1, 1908, should have been of the correct 1.350 inches in diameter and extra thickness. As with the Philadelphia issue, varieties with short and long obverse rays are known and seem to be of about equal availability. (Short Rays—ray immediately above the 8 ends just before the star; Long Rays—ray immediately above the 8 ends past the star.) Differences in ray length might be associated with the new hub made to correct thickness and diameter problems. It is possible the Short Ray varieties are also thinner and slightly wider than their Long Ray counterparts, but to date no studies have been conducted in this area. Revised No Motto dies were distributed in March 1908, followed in late May by new dies including the motto mandated by Congress.

This is a splendidly preserved example that is strongly struck throughout. The bright, frosted surfaces show no obvious abrasions and each side displays rich reddish-golden color with a significant accent of lilac over the highpoints. Only 11 pieces have been so graded (seven by PCGS and four by NGC) with none finer at either service (10/06).
From The Kutasi Collection.(#9143)

Rare MS66 PCGS 1908
With Motto Twenty

3263   1908 Motto MS66 PCGS. Omitting the customary motto IN GOD WE TRUST was not a trivial matter for President Roosevelt. As early as April 1907, he asked Director Roberts for an opinion. According to Roger Burdette's research in the archives: "Roberts replied that it was not required by law, but that the Solicitor of the Treasury said that the motto had been in use for so long that that Congress may have lost the ability to prevent its use." Roosevelt decided to omit the motto on the new gold coin designs and all double eagles and eagles issued in 1907 lacked the motto. This simplified the designs and improved the overall artistic effect.

When the first coins were released in early November 1907, the omission was noticed immediately. Within a few days, letters, telegrams, and petitions peppered the President, Congress, Treasury and the Mint Bureau. Roosevelt issued a lengthy statement explaining his view that, " ... to put such a motto on coins ... does positive harm ... and is in effect irreverence which comes dangerously close to sacrilege ... A beautiful and solemn sentence such as the one in question should be treated and uttered only with that fine reverence which necessarily implies a certain exaltation of spirit." But public sentiment and the Congress were too much behind adding the motto, and by February 20, 1908, the mint had struck a pattern double eagle with the motto on the reverse for Roosevelt to approve. Legislation requiring the motto easily passed Congress and was signed on May 17. By May 23, the mint had made new patterns of both ten and twenty dollar coins for final approval. After June 17, 1908, all the new design gold coins carried the required inscription.

This is a strongly struck example that has rich mint frost and an overlay of beautiful, subtle rose and lilac patina. An outstanding, high grade With Motto twenty and a scarce opportunity to acquire this issue in the ultimate grade. Only 10 other pieces have been so graded by PCGS, and seven others by NGC, with none finer at either service (10/06). It is also interesting to note that Heritage has only offered an MS66 example once before, at the sale of the Phillip H. Morse Collection in November 2005.
From The Kutasi Collection.(#9147)

Sharp 1908-D With Motto
Double Eagle, MS66

3264   1908-D Motto MS66 PCGS. Mint State 1908-D With Motto double eagles are readily available in grades through MS64, partly because of a hoard of several hundred pieces that surfaced in 1983 in Central America. The issue becomes scarce at the Gem level, and is a downright rarity in Premium Gem and better condition. Indeed, PCGS and NGC combined have certified slightly over 20 MS66 examples and a mere five pieces in MS67, with neither service seeing any coins finer.

When the motto IN GOD WE TRUST was added to the lower reverse, the design detail on the master hub was also enhanced. Consequently, the design elements of the 1908-D With Motto are much more sharply defined than those on the typical 1908-D No Motto. The Premium Gem With Motto example in the current lot illustrates these bolder striking impressions in the panes of the Capitol building, on Liberty's facial features, fingers, and toes, and on the eagle's torso feathers. Both sides are awash in vibrant luster that emanates from apricot and peach-gold surfaces accented with subtle lime-green hues. Close inspection reveals just a few trivial marks, none of which are worthy of individual mention. Population: 17 in 66, 3 finer (10/06).

From The Kutasi Collection.(#9148)

Appealing 1908-S Premium Gem Twenty Dollars

3265   1908-S MS66 PCGS. The 1908-S, with a mintage of only 22,000 pieces, has the lowest production of any issue in the Saint-Gaudens series except for the Ultra High Relief and High Relief. Roger Burdette's mint archival research sheds light on reason's for this low mintage: "San Francisco was the last mint to receive dies and collars for the new double eagles. Blueprints were sent from Philadelphia on March 17 and a month later it was discovered that the presses did not have enough clearance to allow the edge collar mechanism to operate. Once the dies were on hand, the mint still had considerable difficulty in adapting their presses to the segmented edge collar. It wasn't until September 10 that double eagles again flowed from the western mint, but they managed to produce only 22,000 of the new coins by year's end."

As with some other San Francisco dates, but unlike many other Saint-Gaudens issues in general, there was apparently an effort to place 1908-S twenties into the channels of commerce, as a larger number of circulated examples than Uncirculated ones are in the marketplace (in this regard, it is instructive to note that PCGS and NGC have to date certified about 460 circulated specimens and approximately 240 Mint State coins). Most Uncirculated pieces grade through MS64. Fewer than 20 Gems are known, and just about 15 Premium Gems and five Superb Gems have been certified.

The MS66 representative we present here displays the thick mint frost and rich orange-gold color that are typical of this issue. Further enhancing the coin's eye appeal is the well-executed strike that manifests itself in the sharply defined features of Liberty, the Capitol building, and the eagle. Much of this sharpness of detail likely comes from a strengthened obverse hub that is seen on twenties beginning with the 1908 With Motto issue. Both sides of this lovely example are impeccably preserved, and reveal no flaws that might be considered detracting. We simply point to a minute mark in the field beneath Liberty's flowing hair and another at the top of the ray closest to her left (right facing) breast, both of which may help to identify the coin.

From The Kutasi Collection.(#9149)

A Rare and Outstanding
1909 Twenty, MS66

3266   1909 MS66 PCGS. Ex: Brahin Collection. In 1909, the Philadelphia Mint struck 162,286 double eagles. Gold authority Roger Burdette writes that 1,104 pieces were rejected and melted, leaving a net mintage of 161,282, which included the 1909/8 overdate. The 1909 is readily available, though not common, in the lower Mint State grades through MS62. MS63 specimens are somewhat more challenging, but higher-grade pieces are seldom seen. David Akers, in his writeup of the 1909 Gem Uncirculated Saint in the Dr. Thaine Price Collection (May 19, 1998, lot 80), discussed the rarity factor of the issue: "Prior to the appearance on the market recently of a substantial number of mint state specimens, the 1909 Saint-Gaudens double eagle was generally considered to be much more scarce than it is now known to be. Hundreds of specimens have come unto the market over the past few years from one large hoard, and many of these specimens are attractive and fairly high quality, although most of them grade Choice Uncirculated or lower. A moderate number, however, are Very Choice Uncirculated, but I am not aware of any that have graded Gem. As a result, although the 1909 is now readily available in Choice Uncirculated, and only moderately rare in Very Choice Uncirculated, Gems like this one are still at the highest rarity level and among the most difficult to obtain in the series." To date (10/06), PCGS and NGC have seen 26 Gems, and 10 MS66 examples; neither service has certified any coins finer.

The Premium Gem in this lot exhibits a bold strike; excellent detail is evident in the panes of the Capitol building, on Liberty's face, on the fingers of both hands, on the toes, as well as on the eagle's torso feathers. Both sides are awash in satiny luster, and are covered in a simply beautiful mix of light orange-gold and mint-green patination. Immaculate preservation is notedthroughout, with no marks indicating the necessity for individual mention. A minute tick on the sun beneath the R in TRUST may help to pedigree the piece. An outstanding coin in every respect, and sure to generate spirited bidding. Population: 5 in 66, 0 finer (10/06).
From The Kutasi Collection.(#9150)

Highly Attractive 1909/8
Gem Double Eagle

3267   1909/8 MS65 PCGS. So far as is known, 1909 was the only year that an overdate was produced in the Saint-Gaudens series of double eagles. Gold specialist Roger Burdette suggests the genesis of this error by noting that working dies for the next calendar year were usually made from October through December of the previous year so that a supply would be ready on January 2. With current-year and next-year hubs in the engraving department, there was ample opportunity for mistakes. Burdette states: "Sometime in late 1908 the die sinkers prepared working dies in the usual manner. This required several strikes (more like "squeezes") from a hydraulic press of the working hub (relief image) to produce a complete working die (incuse image). This process occurred over several days, and for a coin the diameter of a double eagle, may have required a total of four or more strikes to complete a single working die. Evidently, one of the die sinkers accidentally got his hands on a 1908 hub and used that to make some of the impressions. He then switched back to the correct 1909 hub and completed the working die." Burdette goes on to say: "The finished obverse die ... was used and finally discarded. Apparently no one in the coining department realized that a 1909/8 overdate had been created. If they did, no action to condemn the coins was taken."

The 1909/8 represents a considerable challenge above MS63. A little more than 100 near-Gems have been certified by PCGS and NGC. MS65 pieces number about 20, and fewer than 10 coins grade higher. The current Gem specimen displays an apricot-gold color with tints of light green. The luster has a pleasing soft, frosty texture that is common to many Philadelphia coins of this era. While the typical 1909/8 exhibits a general flatness on the obverse, this coin is strongly impressed, as illustrated by excellent definition on Liberty's head, fingers, and toes, and on the Capitol building. The few light contact marks that do occur are well within the parameters of the MS65 grade designation. A highly attractive piece that will not disappoint the new owner. Population: 15 in 65, 3 finer (10/06).
From The Kutasi Collection.(#9151)

Rare 1909-D Premium
Gem Double Eagle

3268   1909-D MS66 PCGS. The 1909-D double eagle, with a mintage of 52,500 pieces, is the fourth lowest production in the series, ranking behind the High Relief, the 1908-S, and the 1913-S. Moreover, most of the 1909-Ds were apparently stored at the Treasury and subsequently melted in the 1930s. Prior to the 1980s, therefore, this issue was considered rarer than the High Relief and the 1913-S, and similar in rarity to the 1908-S. The surfacing of a hoard of double eagles in the early 1980s in Central America lowered the rarity rating of the '09-D, as well as some other dates. In his 1997 book *American Coin Treasures and Hoards,* David Bowers alluded to a commentary from gold specialist David Akers who related to Bowers: "With reference to $20 gold coins from Guatemala or another country in Central America I have knowledge of the pieces dispersed by MTB (Manfra, Tordella & Brookes) in the early 1980s. It is my understanding that there were approximately 47,000 $20 coins in the deal...the majority Uncirculated. The following dates, some previously all but unobtainable, were present in quantity in the deal in Choice to Gem Mint State: 1908-D No Motto, 1908-D With Motto, 1909-D, 1909-S, 1910-S, 1911-S, 1914-S, 1915-S, 1916-S, and 1922-S. ... I sold many ... rolls of individual dates including dozens of Choice Mint State 1909-D. ... "

Along the above lines, Bowers states in his 2004 *A Guide Book of Double Eagle Gold Coins:* "Although the dispersal of several hoards has augmented the supply of Mint State 1909-D double eagles from what it was 20 or 30 years ago, this low-mintage issue is still a highly important key date. Gems are especially rare, and when they come on the market excitement prevails!" His assertion is borne out by the population figures—PCGS and NGC report fewer than 20 1909-D twenties in MS65, three pieces in MS66, and three MS67s.

ThePremium Gem offered in the present lot features a rich apricot-gold color imbued with subtle accents of mint-green. Both sides are enveloped in bright, frosty luster, and exhibit well executed motifs. Most of the panes are visible in the Capitol building, and excellent definition is apparent in Liberty's face, fingers, and toes. The surfaces are devoid of all but a few small abrasions. This is the first Premium Gem example ever offered by Heritage.

From The Kutasi Collection.(#9152)

Elusive 1909-S Twenty, MS66

3269 **1909-S MS66 PCGS.** Gold specialist Roger Burdette, in his research at the National Archives, found that the San Francisco Mint used 13 obverse and 13 reverse dies to strike 2,829,416 double eagles in 1909. He notes that: "Of these, 54,491 (approximately two percent) were rejected by the cadre of lady adjustors who weighed each gold coin. This left a net production of 2,774,925 for commercial use. San Francisco was able to strike an average of 217,647 coins per die pair, or more than nine times the average of the Philadelphia Mint (23,198 per obverse die)."

The 1909-S is relatively obtainable through the near-Gem grade level. As indicated by the PCGS and NGC reports, however, the number of certified pieces drops precipitously from MS64 to MS65. Another significant drop occurs at the Premium Gem level, where the two services have, to date, seen only 13 coins. A single MS67 has also been graded (by PCGS), and neither service has certified any examples finer.

The current Premium Gem 1909-S possesses radiant luster and attractive peach-gold color that is augmented by occasional splashes of slightly deeper orange. Excellent strike definition prevails over the design elements, as revealed in the detail visible in Liberty's fingers on both hands as well as on the face and foot, on the Capitol building, and on the eagle's torso feathers. A few light marks in the field above the eagle's head serve to identify the coin.
From The Kutasi Collection.(#9153)

1910 Condition Rarity
MS66 Double Eagle

3270   1910 MS66 PCGS. The With Motto Saint-Gaudens twenties from the Philadelphia Mint for the years 1908 to 1915 are all at least moderately scarce in all grades. The 1910, with a mintage of 482,167 pieces, is not rare in grades below the Gem level, but is a classic condition rarity in full Gem condition. David Akers, in his 1988 *20th-Century United States Gold Coins, 1907-1933,* writes: "Although not nearly as difficult to locate as the other early Philadelphia Mint issues in Gem condition, the 1910 is definitely rare in MS65, and it takes a little luck and a little patience to be able to find one."

The population reports show a significant drop in 1910 double eagles between the near-Gem and MS65 levels. PCGS and NGC have seen about 1,500 MS64-graded specimens in comparison to approximately 160 or so MS65 pieces. Fewer than 10 Premium Gems have been reported, and none finer.

The typical 1910 Philadelphia-Mint double eagle is very attractive. Akers states: "The 1910 is invariably well struck and the surfaces are always the 'soft' frosty type. Luster on this issue is usually very good (much better than on the 1908 With Motto, 1911, 1913 or 1914) and the color is typically a light to medium yellow or orange gold."

The MS66 coin in this lot displays the usual impressive strike, as evidenced by the sharp detail on Liberty's face, hands, and foot, and on the eagle's plumage. Potent luster embraces both sides, and a classic Kutasi color mix of warm peach-gold, orange-gold, and mint-green adorns frosty, well-preserved surfaces. This original, untampered coin exudes great technical quality and aesthetic appeal, and is sure to delight the new owner. Population: 3 in 66, 0 finer (10/06).
From The Kutasi Collection.(#9154)

Attractive 1910-D Premium Gem Double Eagle

Lovely 1910-S Gem Double Eagle

3271   1910-D MS66 PCGS. Numerous Uncirculated 1910-D double eagles remain from Mint-sewn bags that resided in European banks until sometime after World War II. Most of these grade through MS64, though Gems do occasionally appear on the market. Premium Gems are scarce to rare, and higher-grade pieces are virtually unobtainable, with only three examples certified by PCGS and NGC. This MS66 coin displays excellent definition throughout, which is typical of the issue. The usually seen satiny surfaces possess nice luster and peach-gold color with just the slightest hint of light green undertones. Both sides are remarkably free of mentionable abrasions. An inoffensive linear mark on the lower part of the 8th ray from the left may help to identify the piece. Population: 84 in 66, 2 finer (10/06).

From The Kutasi Collection.(#9155)

3272   1910-S MS65 PCGS. Though the majority of the more than 2.1 million pieces of 1910-S twenties were melted, a hoard of about 100 Uncirculated coins that turned up in a Swiss bank in 1981 and a bag of 1,000 examples that was discovered in Central America in 1983 have made the '10-S a relatively common issue in Mint condition. However, probably no more than 120 Gems are extant today. Above that level, availability drops off quickly. The MS65 in this lot contains light to medium orange-gold luster and well impressed design features. The sharpness of the detail on Liberty's fingers and toes and on the Capitol building is especially noteworthy, and the few small bag marks scattered about are within the confines of the MS65 designation. All in all, a very pretty coin.

From The Kutasi Collection.(#9156)

Sharp 1911 Premium
Gem Double Eagle

3273   1911 MS66 PCGS. The 1911 double eagle, like other Philadelphia-Mint issues from this period, is very scarce in MS65 grades or finer. The higher availability of lower Mint State coins is due to the discovery of a large hoard that is cited by David Akers (1998): "In recent years, a substantial number of decent quality Mint State specimens have appeared on the market from one large hoard, but most of them are only Choice Uncirculated or lower grade specimens."

This Premium Gem example displays bright peach-gold color on highly lustrous surfaces that are somewhat granular, as is typical for the issue. A sharp strike characterizes the design elements, including bold definition on the Capitol building and Liberty's face, hands, and foot. Population: 10 in 66, 0 finer (11/06).
From The Kutasi Collection.(#9157)

Beautiful 1911-D Twenty, MS66

3274 1911-D MS66 PCGS. The 1911-D twenty is readily available in lightly circulated and in Mint State grades through Gem Uncirculated. Premium Gem coins can be obtained with searching and patience, while the date assumes a low R.6 rarity rating in MS67. The current Premium Gem sports an excellent strike, along with the satiny luster and finely granular surfaces common to all double eagles minted from 1909 to 1916. A somewhat variegated pattern of yellow and apricot-gold color envelops both sides, and contact marks are at a minimum. A simply beautiful Denver Mint coin that will not disappoint the new owner.
From The Kutasi Collection.(#9158)

Finest Certified 1911-S Twenty, MS67

3275   1911-S MS67 PCGS. The 1911-S double eagle mint-age was 775,750 pieces. Unlike many later double eagle issues, apparently very few of the '11-S were melted in the 1930s, resulting in thousands of coins being known. Uncirculated examples are readily available through near-Gem, and even MS65 specimens are obtainable with a little patience and searching. A couple of hoards, both of which were recounted in David Bowers' book on *American Coin Treasures and Hoards,* have helped to maintain the fairly large number of low to mid-level Uncirculated 1911-S twenties on the market today. Bowers indicates that sometime in the 1970s, he bought a bag 1911-S double eagles, along with 500-piece bags of 1916-S ten dollar and twenty dollar coins, from a bank officer in Beverly Hills. He states that: "These were subsequently advertised, and were completely sold out within four hours of the time our offering appeared." Bowers also refers to a July 7, 1996, correspondence with gold coin authority David Akers, who indicated that he sold 500 1911-S twenties to one of his customers, that hoard being associated with approximately 47,000 double eagles discovered in Central America in the early 1980s.

As mentioned above, the 1911-S is obtainable through MS65. The number of Premium Gem examples drops off precipitously to fewer than 50 specimens certified by PCGS and NGC. At the MS67 level, only one coin—the present PCGS-graded example—has been reported! The surfaces of this finest-known 1911-S specimen display a granular texture, typical of all 1910-1916 Saints, undoubtedly an influence from the matte proof coins struck during these same years. Both sides are awash with gorgeous apricot-gold luster, tinged with traces of mint-green. The design features are solidly impressed, exhibiting bold definition on the Capitol building, on Liberty's face, fingers, and toes, and on the eagle's feathers. Close inspection with a loupe reveals no mentionable marks, though for accuracy we point out a couple of inoffensive ticks on the right reverse rim. In sum, this is a spectacular coin, sure to draw spirited bidding. Who would not want to own the finest known of anything?

From The Kutasi Collection.(#9159)

Outstanding 1912
Premium Gem Twenty

3276   1912 MS66 PCGS. The 1912 is the only double eagle issue of the year; none were struck at Denver or San Francisco, the first time for a Philadelphia Mint-only twenty since 1886. It is also the first year with 48 obverse stars, reflecting the addition of New Mexico and Arizona into the Union. The issue is fairly available through MS63, but near-Gems become more difficult to locate, and Gems are quite elusive. MS66 pieces, a representative of which we offer here, are nearly unobtainable as evidenced by the PCGS/NGC population data; these services have certified only seven Premium Gems, and none finer.

The 1912 is one of the better-produced dates of the Saint-Gaudens twenty dollar series. Gold specialist David Akers notes that: "The 1912 is always very sharply struck, the most sharply struck of any of the Philadelphia Mint issues from 1907 to 1915. The luster is generally very good to excellent. The surfaces are usually frosty with an occasional specimen having a slightly satiny texture. Color is always very good and is usually a rich yellow-gold, sometimes with a light rose or orange tint. Top grade examples of the 1912 have more eye appeal than any other early Philadelphia Mint issues except the 1915."

The example in this lot largely fits within Akers' description of the "typical" 1912. The strike is powerful, as apparent in the facial features, the fingers, and the toes of Liberty, the panes on the Capitol building, and the feathers on the eagle's torso. The surfaces are frosty and emit glowing luster, and are impeccably preserved, revealing no abrasions worthy of individual mention. The color, while it imparts fantastic eye appeal to the coin, varies a bit from that described by Akers for the typical example. Both sides are apricot-gold with occasional tints of deeper orange and mint-green. This coin is sure to generate considerable enthusiasm and spirited bidding among aficionados of high-grade Saint-Gaudens double eagle coinage. Population: 4 in 66, 0 finer (10/06).
From The Kutasi Collection.(#9160)

Sharp 1913 Gem Double Eagle

3277   1913 MS65 PCGS. The Philadelphia Mint struck 168,780 business strike double eagles in 1913; the issue is one of the major rarities from that facility. Gold specialist David Akers makes reference to the rarity level of this date in his sale of the Dr. Thaine B. Price Collection in 1998: "As a date, the 1913 is much more rare than the 1912; in fact, it is the rarest of the With Motto Philadelphia issues from 1908-1915, especially in Choice Uncirculated or better condition. Gems are prohibitively rare, and for all practical purposes, unobtainable; even in Choice Uncirculated or Very Choice Uncirculated condition, the 1913 is very scarce, if not moderately rare." The certified population more or less substantiates Akers' assertions. Fewer than 700 coins have been graded MS63 by PCGS and NGC combined, and less than 400 have rated near-Gem designation. The break between near-Gem and Gem is significant, as fewer than 15 MS65 coins have been certified by both services, along with one finer!

The 1913 twenty is not considered to be one of the better-produced coins of the Saint-Gaudens double eagle series. Most appear to have the "flat" look of the No Motto issues of 1907 and 1908, and luster is typically below average. Akers sums up the 1913 best when he says: "Even in high grade, the 1913 does not rank with the better looking issues of this type."

The MS65 specimen offered in this lot does not fit the profile of the "typical" 1913. The design elements display a powerful strike, as evidenced by definition on the Capitol building, on Liberty's hand that holds the olive branch and on the toes, as well as on the feathers of the eagle's belly. Vibrant luster emanates from the softly-frosted surfaces that display a pleasing apricot-gold color and are devoid of significant marks. A minute indention on Liberty's left (right-facing) breast and a small unobtrusive scrape on the sun below the W in WE are mentioned as possible pedigree markers. Population: 7 in 65, 0 finer (10/06).

From The Kutasi Collection.(#9161)

Gorgeous 1913-D Gem Twenty

3278   1913-D MS65 PCGS. The 1913-D twenty, with a mintage of 393,500 pieces, can be acquired in most grades without too much difficulty. Mint State coins are plentiful, especially through the near-Gem grade level. MS65 examples are somewhat scarce, but available with patience and searching. Specimens finer than MS65 are far and few between, with a mere 10 pieces certified by PCGS and NGC combined. The current Gem exhibits excellent striking conditions and pretty orange-gold patina imbued with occasional speckles of sky-blue. The finish has a satin-like effect and is devoid of significant marks. A truly gorgeous Gem that will please the connoisseur of Saint-Gaudens coinage.
From The Kutasi Collection.(#9162)

Condition Rarity 1913-S Double Eagle, MS65

3279   1913-S MS65 PCGS. A condition rarity example of this impressive, low mintage issue (34,000 pieces; the third lowest mintage of the series, trailing only the 1908-S and the High Relief). Most pieces have been affected by numerous bagmarks and abrasions from years of storage in a careless manner, but this example is a pleasing exception. The surfaces are most attractive with a bright yellow-golden finish and a nearly mark-free appearance. A single tiny hit is seen at the top of the eagle's leading wing, this being mentioned for future pedigree purposes. Rich, satiny luster completes the picture of this elusive Gem specimen. Population: 17 in 65, 1 finer (10/06).
From The Kutasi Collection.(#9163)

Elusive 1914 Gem Twenty

3280   1914 MS65 PCGS. The 1914, with a mintage of 95,250 pieces, shows a fairly large number of coins in the MS62 to MS64 range, apparently from a large hoard. MS65 and finer examples, however, are elusive. The Gem presented in the current lot has a somewhat frosty finish and attractive apricot-gold color with light gray-green accents. The strike is well executed, as apparent from the nice detail on Liberty's hands and foot and on the eagle's torso. A few minuscule marks on each side preclude a higher grade. Population: 35 in 65, 3 finer (10/06).
From The Kutasi Collection.(#9164)

Challenging 1914-D Premium Gem Double Eagle

3281   1914-D MS66 PCGS. Many of the 453,000 1914-D double eagles escaped the melting pots of the 1930s, and the issue is now considered a relatively common date of the Saint-Gaudens series. In Premium Gem, however, it becomes more elusive, and is virtually unobtainable above MS66. This specimen displays beautiful orange-gold luster with some lighter shades scattered throughout, and a relatively bold strike is noted on the design features. A small linear abrasion on Liberty's forehead is mentioned for accuracy. Population: 45 in 66, 1 finer (10/06).
From The Kutasi Collection.(#9165)

Pleasing 1914-S MS66 Twenty

3282   1914-S MS66 PCGS. The large mintage of the 1914-S double eagle (nearly 1.5 million pieces) is a good indicator of its availability, unlike many issues of the Saint-Gaudens series. It apparently escaped the mass meltings of the 1930s, as evidenced by the several thousand examples that have been certified by the grading services. Premium Gem coins, however, such as the one described here, do not show up as often, and higher grade pieces are virtually unobtainable. Apricot-gold surfaces display radiant luster and sharply executed motifs, and the few minor marks on each side do not betray the MS66 designation. A nice all-around coin. Population: 62 in 66, 0 finer (10/06).
From The Kutasi Collection.(#9166)

Flashy 1915 Gem Twenty

3283   1915 MS65 PCGS. The 1915 Philadelphia double eagle, with a mintage of 152,000 business strikes, is moderately scarce in all grades. As can be seen from the certified population, It becomes rare in MS65, and virtually unobtainable in higher levels of preservation. Approximately 60 pieces have been given the MS65 grade designation by PCGS and NGC combined, and none have been seen finer! As is generally the case with the 1915, the design features on the Gem in this lot are boldly executed; the fingers on both hands are completely separated, as are the toes, the panes on the Capitol building, and the feathers on the eagle's torso. Vibrant luster radiates from rich apricot-gold surfaces that reveal fewer marks than one might expect for a large, heavy gold coin assigned an MS65 designation. Population: 25 in 65, 0 finer (10/06).
From The Kutasi Collection.(#9167)

Marvelous 1915-S Double Eagle, MS66

3284   1915-S MS66 PCGS. Radiantly lustrous surfaces that display an attractive peach-gold patina highlighted with subtle champagne and lavender accents are the first attribute of this marvelous Premium Gem to greet the eyes of the viewer. These are complemented by boldly impressed design elements that reveal startling definition, especially on Liberty's face and fingers, on the olive branch, and on the eagle's feathers. A few light marks are well within the confines of the MS66 grade designation. 1915-S twenties grading finer are virtually unobtainable.

From The Kutasi Collection.(#9168)

Challenging 1916-S Premium Gem Double Eagle

3285   1916-S MS66 PCGS. The surfaces of this Premium Gem display the pleasing fine granularity that is characteristic of the 1916-S twenty. Peach-gold patina overlies glowing luster, and is imbued with traces of yellow-gold and light green. The design features reveal an impressive strike, manifesting itself in sharp detail on Liberty's face, hands, and foot, and on the olive branch and eagle's breast. A few trivial marks do not distract. The availability of MS66 coins drops precipitously with approximately one-tenth the number certified when compared to MS65 examples.

From The Kutasi Collection.(#9169)

Finest PCGS-Certified
Gem 1920 Double Eagle

3286   1920 MS65 PCGS. Ex: Eliasberg. Between 1916 and 1920 no double eagles were struck by the U.S. Mint. When double eagle production was resumed in May 1920, gold specialist Roger Burdette writes that the coins were intended to remain in the Treasury Department reserves and not be released for commercial use. Burdette cites a letter dated May 5, 1920, from T. Louis Comparette, curator of the Philadelphia Mint coin collection, to George Godard, Connecticut State Librarian, that discusses the 1920 issue. Comparette wrote: "Herewith I am sending you a twenty dollar gold piece, just struck. This is the first gold to be struck since 1916. It is for the Reserve Funds and not to be issued for general circulation, and the securing of the specimens for others than the government collection is probably irregular, so please do not let the fact become public knowledge. For others will demand specimens as soon as they learn that a few have them. That might cause embarrassment." Burdette notes that Comparette reinforced the rarity of the 1920 double eagle in a December 7 letter: "... But very few of them got out. All the rest are under seal along with the reserve funds, and the repeated efforts of scores to secure specimens have so far proved unavailing. ... I have been offered as high as $30 for a specimen. ... Sometime, undoubtedly, they will be obtainable, but nobody can surmise when."

The 1920 is available through MS63, but becomes more challenging at the near-Gem level. In Gem condition, the 1920 is one of the most, if not *the* most underrated condition rarity in the entire series of Saint-Gaudens twenties. Only eight pieces have been so graded (one by PCGS, and seven by NGC) with none finer at either service. This is an absolutely splendid coin that has rich mint frost and peach-gold coloration accented with splashes of delicate mint-green. The design elements are well defined, as illustrated by the detail on the Capitol building, on Liberty's face, fingers, and toes, on the olive branch, and on the eagle's feathers. A few light marks fall well within the parameters of the MS65 designation. A minute abrasion on the top curve of the 9 in the date may aid in identification of the coin. This is a rare opportunity for the specialist, and for the collector who only wants PCGS-certified Gems this is the only chance to obtain this date.
From The Kutasi Collection.(#9170)

1920-S DOUBLE EAGLE, MS64 PCGS

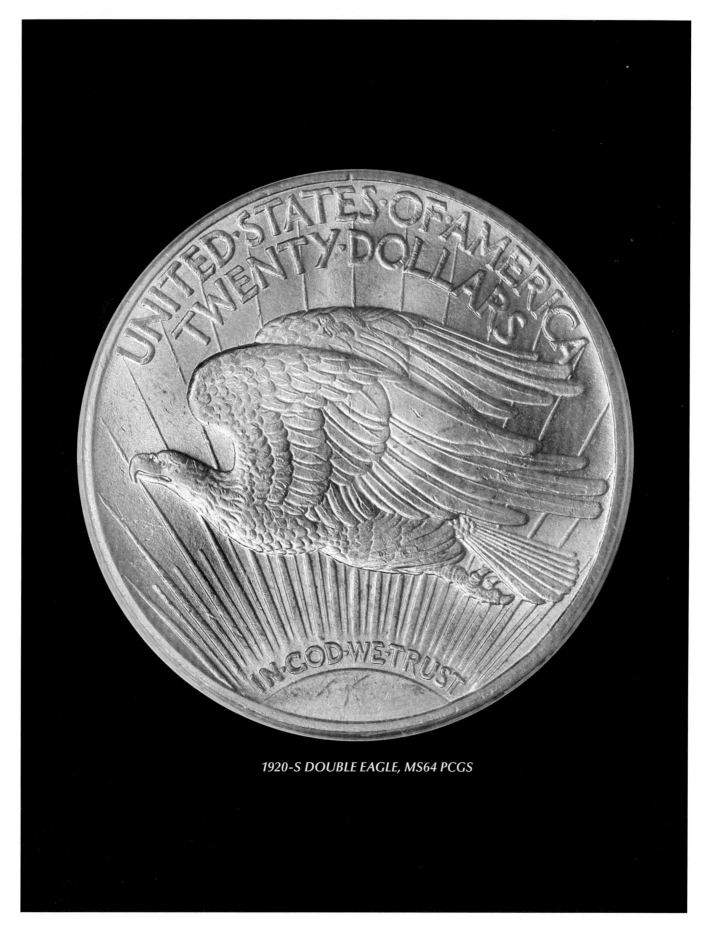

1920-S DOUBLE EAGLE, MS64 PCGS

Elusive 1920-S Near-Gem Double Eagle

3287   1920-S MS64 PCGS. The 1920-S double eagle, with an original mintage of 558,000 pieces, has never been readily available. Most were apparently kept in government vaults until the 1930s, when nearly the entire mintage seems to have been melted. Gold specialist David Akers nicely summarizes the rarity of the 1920-S twenty in his catalog of the Dr. Thaine B. Price Collection (1998): "The 1920-S is one of the major rarities of the Saint-Gaudens series. All grades considered, probably no more than 80-100 examples exist and the majority of them are circulated with XF to AU specimens being typical. In the lowest mint state grades below Choice Uncirculated, the 1920-S is rare and seldom available, and in grades of Choice Uncirculated and Very Choice Uncirculated, the 1920-S is very rare. Gems are exceedingly rare with only 3-4 examples known, placing the 1920-S near the top of the Saint-Gaudens Double Eagle series with respect to condition rarity. In fact, only the 1921 Double Eagle is more rare in Very Choice or Gem Uncirculated condition than the 1920-S, although, of course, in overall population rarity, the 1920-S also does not compare to the 1927-D and 1907 Extremely High Relief. The 1920-S has been regarded as a rare issue since as far back as the 1930's, but it was not until quite a few years later that it was recognized as one of the premier rarities of the series. In the 1940's, the 1920-S was overshadowed by such issues as the 1921, 1924-S, 1925-D, 1926-D, 1926-S, 1927-D, 1927-S, 1930-S and 1931-D among others. However, unlike most of those issues, to the best of my knowledge, no hoard or even small group of this issue has ever been found. In fact, except for an occasionally newly discovered circulated piece, the known population of this issue has remained relatively unchanged for decades." With regard to this last point, David Bowers, in his 2004 *A Guide Book of Double Eagle Gold Coins,* states that: "Unlike some of the rarities of later years in the decade, the supply of 1920-S has not been augmented by hundreds or thousands of recent imports."

PCGS/NGC population data generally corroborate Akers' estimates of extant 1920-S double eagles. To date (10/06), the above two services have certified only 144 '20-S twenties in all grades, some coins of which have likely been resubmitted. Of this number, 95 are Uncirculated, and only 34 have achieved the near-Gem or finer grade levels. Two examples are off the market: a Superb Gem in the American Numismatic Society cabinet, and a Smithsonian piece that grades "at least MS64" (Jeff Garrett and Ron Guth, *Encyclopedia of U.S. Gold Coins, 1795-1933,* 2006).

The near-Gem specimen presented in this lot displays bright peach-gold surfaces that are imbued with just the slightest hint of mint-green undertones. Strike can be a problem on most 1920-S double eagles, and some minor softness is noted on the Capitol building of this example. All in all, though, the design features exhibit nice definition, particularly on the fingers of both hands, on the olive branch, and on the eagle's breast feathers. Both sides are well preserved, and appear to reveal fewer marks than what might be expected for the MS64 grade designation. A couple of minute contact marks on the reverse sun may help to pedigree this particular coin. Population: 16 in 64, 4 finer (10/06).
From The Kutasi Collection.(#9171)

Rare 1921 Near-Gem Double Eagle

3288   1921 MS64 PCGS. The 1921 is a classic rarity in the Saint-Gaudens double eagle series. It is comparable in overall rarity to the 1920-S, but is considerably more challenging as a condition rarity, especially in the better grades of Uncirculated. A few more coins in the XF-AU grade range are known of the 1921 (about 70 1921 specimens have been certified XF-AU by PCGS and NGC, as contrasted to approximately 50 XF-AU examples of the 1920-S), but there are only a handful of 1921 coins extant above MS63 (specifically, the services have graded eight near-Gem and finer 1921 specimens, and 34 1920-S MS64 and better coins).

The reported mintage of the 1921 was 528,000 pieces, which is lower-than-average for the 1920s era, when totals of one million or more coins were common. Nevertheless, the figure was not so low as to suggest that the issue would be a tough date. In this regard, Paul Green, in an August 15, 2006 *Numismatic News* article entitled "1921 Double Eagle Survives in Low Numbers," writes: "The 1921 was more than a decade before the Gold Recall Order and the melting that followed. It's easy to understand why a date in the 1930s might have been heavily melted, but it's less easy to figure out why the 1921 would have been melted in large numbers. After all, a number of dates produced after 1921 show little evidence of being heavily destroyed in the recall. The 1923, for example, had a nearly identical mintage (566,000 pieces), but there is no evidence of unusual melting...yet the 1923 is $850 in VF20, but the 1921 is priced at $12,000."

Continued on next page

Rare 1921 Near-Gem Double Eagle

Approximately half of the extant 1921 double eagle population is located at the circulated grade levels, prompting Green to say: "The circulated numbers seen at both grading services suggest that the 1921 had a rather routine period, with some coins being released, although probably not all. There is reason to believe that a small number went overseas." If some of this issue did in fact go overseas, it must have been very small, as no appreciable hoards of the 1921 double eagle are known. Indeed, Walter Breen, in his 1988 *Encyclopedia of U.S. and Colonial Coins,* refers to "...about 5 from European sources since 1981." Along a similar vein, David Bowers, in his discussion of the 1921 in his 2004 treatise *A Guide Book of Double Eagle Gold Coins,* states: "While some have sneaked into the market in recent years, and offerings of the past decade are more numerous than in earlier times, no quantities of hundreds or more Mint State pieces have turned up, unlike the case for certain former rarities later in the decade."

The 1921 twenty was notably absent from the Dr. Thaine Price Collection, and that in the Browning Collection was a Choice AU. The Harry Bass and Henry Norweb collections each contained an MS63 example, and the Phillip Morse Collection included an MS64, an MS65, and an MS66. And according to Jeff Garrett and Ron Guth in their 2006 *Encyclopedia of U.S. Gold Coins, 1795-1933,* "...both the American Numismatic Society and the Smithsonian collection contain a superb Gem example of the date. Both were obtained from the Mint at the time of issue."

This Near-Gem survivor displays a satiny overall sheen and strong cartwheel luster effects. An impressive strike is noted on the design elements, manifesting itself in strong definition on the Capitol building, on Liberty's face and on the fingers of the left hand and the associated olive branch, and on most of the eagle's plumage. Rich green-gold and orange-gold colors blend together over the surfaces. Several scattered abrasions are not unusual for the assigned grade; a minute diagonal mark in the left obverse field and a couple more on the reverse sun are mentioned solely to help aid for future pedigree purposes. This is an important bidding opportunity for either the double eagle or 20th century gold specialist. Housed in an earlier PCGS holder with a green insert. Population: 3 in 64, 3 finer (10/06).
From The Kutasi Collection.(#9172)

Condition Rarity 1922
Premium Gem Twenty

3289   1922 MS66 PCGS. The 1922 Philadelphia double eagle, with a mintage of nearly 1.4 million pieces, largely escaped the gold recall order of 1933. The principal reason for this, according to David Bowers (2004), was that "Vast quantities of 1922-dated double eagles were exported in the 1920s (presumably to Europe) and remained there until after World War II." Consequently, the 1922 is common through the MS64 grade level. MS65 coins become a bit more difficult, but are available with a little patience and searching. There is a precipitous drop, however, in the certified population from Gem to MS66 (specifically, from more than 1,200 MS65 coins to only 16 MS66 pieces), with none finer having been seen by either grading service.

This Premium Gem displays pretty apricot-gold patina with subtle greenish tints and exceptionally attractive luster. A well-executed strike shows itself in strong definition on Liberty's face, fingers, and toes, and on the eagle's breast feathers. The surfaces have a frosty finish, and are well preserved. A few "chatter" marks on the lower part of the torch may help to identify the piece. Population: 7 in 66, 0 finer (10/06).
From The Kutasi Collection.(#9173)

Rare 1922-S Double Eagle, MS65

3290   1922-S MS65 PCGS. Most of the 2.685 million-piece mintage of the 1922-S double eagle was likely retained in the United States and subsequently melted. However, some were also exported; Walter Breen (1988) noted: "At least 7,000 Uncs. turned up in Central America, 1983." With regard to Breen's assertion, David Bowers, in his *American Coin Treasures and Hoards,* quotes a July 7, 1996 letter from gold authority David Akers, who says of the 1922-S: "Only a few hundred coins were found, some of which were of high quality." In any event, high-grade Uncirculated 1922-S examples are a rarity. Fewer than 20 MS65 specimens have been certified by PCGS and NGC, and a mere five are reported finer (all in MS66).

The Premium Gem featured in the current lot exhibits potent luster exuded from gorgeous peach-gold surfaces, as well as sharply impressed motifs; bold delineation is seen on the fingers of Liberty's hands and on her face. A few minute marks preclude an even higher grade. Population: 8 in 65, 2 finer (10/06).
From The Kutasi Collection.(#9174)

Dazzling 1923-D Superb Gem Twenty

3292   1923-D MS67 PCGS. The 1923-D, with a mintage just over 1.7 million pieces, is one of the most readily obtainable issues in the Saint-Gaudens series. Even MS66 coins are available with relatively little trouble. The situation changes at the MS-67 level, where only about 85 coins have been seen by PCGS and NGC combined, and a single piece finer. The current Superb Gem radiates dazzling luster, and is graced with gorgeous apricot-gold color imbued with traces of light green. Excellent detail on the design features has resulted from a powerful strike, and both sides are impeccably preserved. Population: 55 in 67, 0 finer (10/06).
From The Kutasi Collection.(#9176)

Exquisite 1924 Twenty, MS67

One of Three Finest Certified
1923 Double Eagles, MS66

3291   1923 MS66 PCGS. The 1923 Philadelphia-issue twenty, like its 1922-P counterpart, was spared the mass meltings of the 1930s, most likely because many 1920s-dated double eagles resided in overseas banks. Several thousand pieces have been certified through the MS64 grade level, but MS65 coins are very elusive in comparison to the demand for them. MS66 examples are nearly unobtainable, with a mere three coins having been certified by PCGS, and none by NGC; neither service has reported any 1923-Ps finer.

The coin offered here is one of the three known MS66 specimens. Another is currently in the Duckor Collection, and another was sold by Heritage out of the Philip Morse Collection, on November 3, 2005, where it realized $48,875. The present example may well be the finest known. It yields rich, softly frosted luster that radiates through a subtle blend of peach and orange-gold patination. The design elements are powerfully impressed, including excellent definition on Liberty's face and on the hand grasping the olive branch. Nicely preserved surfaces reveal no more than the expected occasional mark. A series of minuscule "chatter" marks beneath the N of TWENTY helps to identify this particular coin.
From The Kutasi Collection.(#9175)

3293   1924 MS67 PCGS. The 1924, with a mintage of more than 4 million examples, is believed to be the most common of the entire Saint-Gaudens double Eagle series. Evidently, virtually the entire issue was sent overseas for international banking transactions. Tens of thousands of coins have been certified through Premium Gem, after which the population drops off dramatically. Excellent luster is visible on the current MS67 specimen, and variegated orange-gold and mint-green patina dances over both sides. An exquisite strike manifests itself in bold delineation on the panes of the Capitol building, as well as on Liberty's facial features, the fingers of both hands, on the foot, and on the eagle's plumage. Impeccable preservation is noted throughout. Population: 71 in 67, 1 finer (10/06).
From The Kutasi Collection.(#9177)

1924-D Condition Rarity
Twenty Dollar, MS65

3294   1924-D MS65 PCGS. Although minted in sufficient numbers (over 3 million pieces), David Bowers, in his *Guide Book of Double Eagle Gold Coins,* (2004) writes that: "Most were probably retained in the United States and melted in the mid-1930s. However, at least a couple thousand were exported. Today, the 1924-D is quite scarce." The typical survivor is rather heavily abraded and most often grades from high-end AU through mid-grade Uncirculated. A coin grading MS64 is about as nice as a collector can hope to acquire, as examples in better condition are far and few between (PCGS and NGC have to date certified 15 Gems, and only three pieces finer). Moreover, the issue varies in striking quality, perhaps because of what Bowers suggests: "The dies seem to have been kept in service for a long time during the production runs for this high-mintage date."

The MS65 example being offered here displays an above-average strike, particularly in the peripheral areas, and on the fingers of Liberty's left (right-facing) hand, on her toes, and on the eagle's breast feathers. Intense luster and apricot-gold patina accented with traces of lime-green adorns the surfaces on both sides. A few very minor marks scattered about do not distract and are mentioned solely for the sake of accuracy. A minute mark on the sun beneath the N of IN will help to pedigree the piece. Population: 5 in 65, 2 finer (11/06).
From The Kutasi Collection.(#9178)

Impressively Struck 1924-S Twenty, MS64

3295 **1924-S MS64 PCGS.** The 1924-S twenty, with a mintage of nearly 3 million pieces, was one of the most heavily melted issues in the series. In fact, almost all of the survivors came from French and Swiss banks. Bowers (2004) states: "... following the tapping of overseas hoards, the 1924-S remains elusive, but enough exist that they come on the market with regularity, usually in lower Mint State grades."

The MS64 example presented here exhibits an impressive strike, especially on the fingers of both of Liberty's hands, on the toes, and on the eagle's feathers. Glowing luster emanates from both sides, which assume apricot and brass-gold patina imbued with traces of light tan. A few light contact marks do not detract from the overall eye appeal. Population: 79 in 64, 3 finer (10/06).
From The Kutasi Collection.(#9179)

Condition Rarity 1925 Double Eagle, MS67

3296 **1925 MS67 PCGS.** The 1925 double eagle is readily obtainable in grades through MS66. This high availability results in part from the high original mintage of 2.83 million pieces, as well as to their long-term residence in foreign banks during the domestic melts of the 1930s. David Bowers (2004) says that "...foreign hoards provided the source for most examples in the hands of numismatists and investors." Superb Gem examples, such as the one we offer here, run counter to the ready obtainability of lower Mint State coins. Indeed, PCGS and NGC report a paltry 11 1925 double eagles, and none finer!

This specimen displays appealing attributes that are characteristic of the date. Exceptionally well preserved, frost-like surfaces are awash in coruscating luster and gorgeous peach-gold patination and light green undertones. Impeccably struck design features exhibit sharp detail in the Capitol building, on Liberty's face, fingers, and toes, and throughout the eagle's plumage. The aficionado of high-grade Saint-Gaudens coinage will not want to miss out on one of the finest known 1925 double eagles. Population: 5 in 67, 0 finer (10/06).
From The Kutasi Collection.(#9180)

Among Finest Certified 1925-D Double Eagles

3297   1925-D MS66 PCGS. Nearly 3 million double eagles were struck at the Denver facility in 1925. Many of these were sent to Europe, primarily to Swiss and French banks, as exchange payments. These represented the bulk of the coins that escaped the melting pots of the 1930s. According to David Bowers in his book *American Coin Treasures and Hoards:* "During the late nineteenth and early twentieth centuries Swiss and other foreign banks were not the slightest bit interested in holding United States paper money, and when President Franklin D. Roosevelt called in gold coins in 1933-1934, Swiss and other banks held on to their gold reserves more tightly than ever."

With respect to rarity, gold specialist David Akers, in his treatise entitled *A Handbook of 20th Century United States Gold Coins, 1907-1933,* states: "In most respects, the 1925-D is very similar in rarity to the 1924-D although, in my experience, it is slightly rarer than the 1924-D in the highest Mint State grades. At one time, the 1925-D was considered to be a major rarity, much more rare than the 1920-S, 1930-S, 1931 and 1932, among others. A few small hoards were subsequently discovered and, even today, there is reportedly a small hoard intact of perhaps as many as 80 to 100 pieces. However, it is likely that the total number of Mint State pieces in existence is still fewer than 200. Most of the known Mint State pieces are MS63 or less and in MS64 condition, the 1925-D is extremely difficult to locate. I have seen a very few small number of true gems, maybe as many as four or five, and I assume that others exist, hence my R-8 rarity rating."

Continued on next page

Among Finest Certified 1925-D Double Eagles

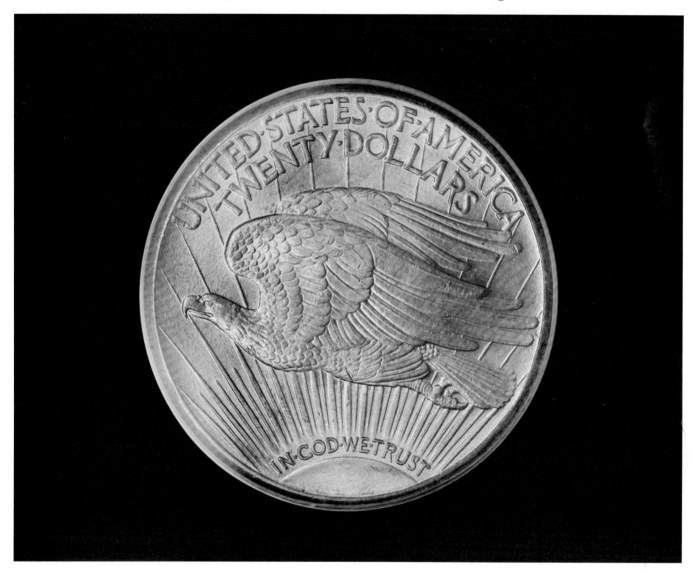

In light of current PCGS and NGC population statistics (in which about 500 Mint State coins have been seen), Akers' estimates of "fewer than 200" Uncirculated 1925-D pieces extant was likely somewhat off (though many examples in the certified population are presumably resubmissions). His estimate of surviving "true Gems," however, is very much in line with the population data - only 10 MS65 coins have been certified, and a mere three MS66 specimens, with none finer.

An impressive strike emboldens the design elements of this Premium Gem example; sharp detail is apparent in the Capitol building, in Liberty's face, on the fingers of both hands, on the toes, and on the eagle's plumage. Both sides exhibit frosted surfaces that radiate intense luster and are adorned with varying shades of apricot and yellow-gold color imbued with traces of mint-green. A couple of minute marks on the torch may help in identification of this lovely specimen that is among the finest known. Population: 2 in 66, 0 finer (11/06). *From The Kutasi Collection.*(#9181)

1925-S Condition Rarity Twenty Dollar, MS65, One of the Finest Known

3298   1925-S MS65 PCGS. Ex: Crawford. When one considers mintmarked double eagles from the 1920s, it is often the case that the original mintages are nearly irrelevant and have little or nothing to do with the surviving population of a particular issue. This generalization applies to the 1925-S that saw 3,776,500 pieces struck, the third highest production run in the entire 54-coin series, and a figure that belies the true rarity of this issue. The vast majority of the production run was apparently melted in the 1930s, and only 600 or so coins are believed known today in all grades, making it one of the major rarities in the Saint-Gaudens series. In their book, *Encyclopedia of U.S. Gold Coins, 1795-1933,* Jeff Garrett and Ron Guth write of the 1925-S: "Those that did survive can likely be traced back to the meager hoards held by European banks, or they were squirreled away by fortunate American collectors."

The 1925-S refutes another commonly held notion about this series, namely, that twenty dollar gold pieces played no role in the 1920s medium of exchange. From the grade distribution of the certified population, it appears that some attempt was made to actually use the 1925-S in the channels of commerce. About 300 circulated coins, especially in XF and AU condition, have been seen by PCGS and NGC, nearly as many pieces that occur in the Mint State grade levels.

Continued on next page

When we combine the extensive meltings from the 1930s with an attempt to circulate the '25-S, the issue emerges as one of the premier condition rarities in the series, along with the 1924-S and 1926-D. Only 30 or so certified pieces have been seen in near-Gem or better condition. Perhaps most important to its status as a key date in the series, the 1925-S is also one of the few issues from the 1920s that never was found in large hoards in Europe.

The Gem example that we offer in the current lot displays radiant luster that exudes from immaculately preserved surfaces. A mixture of peach-gold and lime-green patina rests over both sides, and the design features are exquisitely brought up, including bold detail on Liberty's face, hands, foot, most of the Capitol building, and on the eagle's feathers. A few minor marks beneath the G in GOD will help to pedigree the piece for future collectors. The savvy collector of Saint-Gaudens coinage will not want to miss out on this lovely Gem. Gold specialist David Akers, in his *Handbook of 20th Century United ed States Gold Coins,* listed this coin as the third finest he had seen, "...a satiny specimen in the 1987 F.U.N sale that was purchased by Dr. William Crawford. Despite a few hairlines, it is an exceptional coin, virtually free of bagmarks, with wonderful luster and color." Population: 2 in 65, 3 finer (11/06).
From The Kutasi Collection.(#9182)

Sharply Struck 1926
Premium Gem Twenty

3299   1926 MS66 PCGS. A significant number of 1926-P double eagles were saved in European banks, making this date one of the most common issues in the Saint-Gaudens twenty dollar series. Thousands of coins have been certified by PCGS and NGC through the MS65 grade level. The 1926 becomes somewhat more challenging in MS66, and is extremely rare any finer. Greenish-gold luster radiates from lovingly preserved surfaces, and a well-executed strike emboldens the design elements.
From The Kutasi Collection.(#9183)

1926-D Condition Rarity
Double Eagle, MS65

3300   1926-D MS65 PCGS. The Denver Mint struck 481,000 double eagles in 1926. Most of these were apparently retained in the United States and subsequently melted in the 1930s. Few if any seem to have been sent overseas, as no hoards or significant accumulations have been discovered.

The rarity status of the 1926-D is cogently described by David Akers in his cataloging of the Gem Uncirculated example in the Dr. Thaine Price Collection: "The 1926-D is one of the premier condition rarities of the Saint-Gaudens double eagle series. In most respects it is comparable to the 1925-S, although if anything, it is even more difficult to locate above Choice Uncirculated condition than the 1925-S. Along with the 1924-S, the 1926-D is one of only two Saint-Gaudens double eagles that, as of the writing of this catalog (May 1998), has never been certified as a Gem by at least one of the major grading services. In my opinion, however, that is likely to change once the Price specimens offered here are sold, depending on whether or not the new owners decide to 'slab' them." In the ensuing years, PCGS has certified five MS65 examples and two MS66 coins; NGC has yet to see Gem or finer specimens. It is also noteworthy in this regard that the '26-D has, to the best of our knowledge, made only eight appearances in MS65 or better grades through the major auction firms in the last 15 or so years.

The Gem example presented here displays dazzling luster that radiates from peach and yellow-gold surfaces tinged with traces of light tan and greenish-gray. A sharp strike occurs on the design elements, save for the usual softness in the Capitol dome. A wispy linear mark in the upper left obverse border serves to identify this marvelous piece that is sure to command keen bidder interest.

From The Kutasi Collection.(#9184)

Flashy 1926-S Gem Twenty Dollar

3301 1926-S MS65 PCGS. Jeff Garrett and Ron Guth (2006) write: "...the 1926-S double eagle suffered the same fate as its Denver brother of the same year. The rather impressive mintage (2,041,500 pieces) was all but obliterated from the public's hands, though a few have turned up in overseas bank hoards." A thousand or so Mint State coins have been reported by PCGS and NGC in the MS60 to MS64 range. Gems are elusive, however, with fewer than 40 coins certified, along with a mere seven finer.

The MS65 1926-S example in the current lot displays "flashy" apricot-gold surfaces with a frost-like finish. Sharply defined motifs are apparent on Liberty's face and in the fingers of both hands, as well as on the eagle's feathers. A small linear mark to the right of the Y in LIBERTY may aid in identifying the piece for pedigree purposes. Population: 19 in 65, 2 finer (10/06).
From The Kutasi Collection.(#9185)

Outstanding 1927 Superb Gem Twenty

3302 1927 MS67 PCGS. The 1927, with its mintage of nearly 3 million pieces, is the second most common issue in the series, trailing only the 1924. To date, the certified population approaches 200,000 coins! An abrupt break in the population occurs between MS66 and MS67, with the former grade showing more than 5,000 examples certified, and the latter only 40, with none higher! The condition scarcity MS67 piece in this lot displays bright mint frost and outstanding luster, and is adorned with gorgeous apricot-gold color accented with mint-green. Crisp detail prevails on the design elements, and the surfaces are devoid of mentionable marks. Population: 12 in 67, 0 finer (10/06).
From The Kutasi Collection.(#9186)

1927-D DOUBLE EAGLE, MS66 PCGS

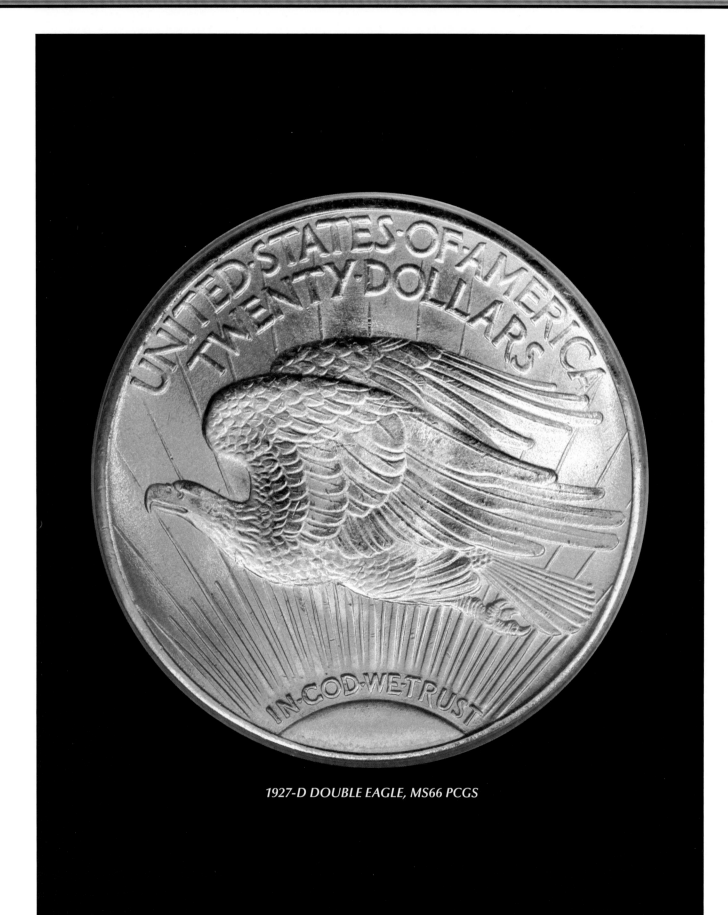

1927-D DOUBLE EAGLE, MS66 PCGS

Legendary 1927-D Double Eagle, MS66

3303   1927-D MS66 PCGS. The 1927-D double eagle is considered to be the rarest United States gold coin of the 20th century. Its closest rival is the 1907 Ultra High Relief. However, more examples are known of the Ultra than of the 1927-D. Moreover, many consider the Ultra to be a pattern issue.

Jeff Garret and Ron Guth, in their *Encyclopedia of U.S. Gold Coins, 1795-1933,* present an interesting scenario on the potential elevation of the 1927-D's rarity status: "The 1927-D double eagle is legendary, and has earned its status as the rarest regular-issue gold coin of any denomination of the 20th century. Only the 1933 double eagle comes close in terms of the number known. However, if the current lawsuit over the ownership of another 10 examples of the 1933 double eagle resolves favorably for collectors, that date will fall into second place behind the 1927-D issue. After decades of contention, it appears that the 1927-D double is truly the king of all 20th century gold coins." Of course, only time will tell whether or not all of this will materialize.

The 1927-D twenty had a relatively low mintage of 180,000 pieces. This alone, however, does not account for its rarity, that is more a function of its very low survival rate. The 1927-D was extensively melted in the 1930s, virtually annihilating the entire production run. *Coin World* staff writer Eric von Klinger, in an article entitled "Collectors Learned Only Slowly of True Rarity of 1927-D Gold $20," writes: "The presumption has been that many 1927-D Saint-Gaudens double eagles had never been issued, or were disproportionately turned in, when President Franklin D. Roosevelt issued his gold surrender order of 1933. They were then melted with other gathered-up gold coins." von Klinger goes on to say: "It can be doubted whether any 1927-D Saint-Gaudens double eagles ever actually circulated. It appears that all known examples are Mint State and of 'choice' or 'gem' quality....Almost the entire mintage may have stayed in government vaults until the later meltings, and only examples requested by collectors or others have survived." Along this line, David Bowers, in his *Guide Book of Double Eagle Gold Coins: A Complete History and Price Guide,* remarks that: "Interestingly, double eagles of this date and mint were available for face value from the Treasury Department from 1927 to the early 1930s."

In his May 19, 1998 write-up of the Gem Uncirculated double eagle in the Dr. Thaine B. Price Collection (lot 115), David Akers commented on the rarity status of the 1927-D: "Today, the 1927-D double eagle is widely and correctly regarded as the rarest regular issue Saint-Gaudens double eagle from 1907-1932. However, when it (the Price specimen) was purchased in the 1940s by the Auction '84 consignor, 'Mr. Lima,' that was definitely not the case, and although the 1927-D was considered to be an important rarity in the series, it was generally thought to be in the second tier of Saint-Gaudens rarities below such dates as 1921, 1924-S, 1926-S, 1926-D, 1927-S, and 1931-D. However, in the intervening half century, at least small quantities of all of those other issues have been discovered, mostly overseas in European banks, but, to the best of my knowledge, there has not been a single additional 1927-D located that was not already known to collectors by 1950."

Relatively few specimens of the 1927-D are known. Again in the Price catalog, Akers wrote: "There have been occasions in the past where somewhat exaggerated claims of this issue's rarity have been made; some have even claimed that only 6-8 pieces are known. Actually, there are considerably more known than that, and I would place the number extant in the range of 12-15 pieces, making the 1927-D very similar in overall rarity to the 1907 Extremely High Relief, if not just slightly more rare. I have personally examined 12 different examples of the 1927-D double eagle, and since there are a few auction records for pieces that I cannot match with the specimens that I am familiar with, I feel that it is likely that a few more exist than just the 12 I have seen. I think it is conservative and accurate to say that any sale containing a 1927-D double eagle is a major numismatic event."

In one of his prior works, *A Handbook of 20th-Century United States Gold Coins, 1907-1933,* (1988), Akers referred to the grade levels of surviving 1927-D double eagles: "The majority are MS63 or better and several are solid Gems. The Eliasberg coin now owned by a prominent eastern collector is a high-end MS65, and the Dr. Steven Duckor example which he purchased from Auction '84 and the Browning Collection specimen are both full MS65. The three examples in the Smithsonian Institution are all MS63 to MS64 as is the coin from Stack's October 1985 sale that was purchased by MTB for a client. It is difficult to pick out one piece as the "finest" but that accolade most likely should go to the Eliasberg specimen."

Population data from the grading services may shed some light on the number of extant 1927-D double eagles. To date (11/06), PCGS and NGC have graded a total of 12 examples (some of these, of course, may be resubmissions). PCGS-graded coins include an MS63, an MS65, four MS66 pieces, and an MS67. NGC has seen an AU58, an MS65, and three MS66 specimens. And Bowers, in his *Guide Book,* suggests that one or two 1927-D examples exist in the "circulated field population," along with 12 to 15 pieces in the "Mint State field population" (Bowers defines circulated field population as the "Author's estimate of the number of existing double eagles in all circulated grades from Fine or less, to AU58," and Mint State field population as the "Author's estimate of the total number of double eagle's in Mint State, all grades combined from MS60 upward, existing in the hands of collectors and investors. No account is made for undiscovered hoards, if any exist."

Auction records and private treaty sales may also help to elucidate the number of surviving 1927-D double eagle specimens. Listings of these have been presented in rosters developed by various numismatists over the years. We have attempted to update the roster of '27-D's by comparing photographs of the appearances of these coins in catalogs that were readily accessible to us. This updated roster is presented below:

1. Smithsonian specimen, acquired from Denver Mint in 1927.

2. Smithsonian specimen, acquired from Denver Mint in 1927.

3. J.F. Bell specimen sold by Stack's, lot 1004, December 1944 for $500; this was apparently the earliest auction appearance of a 1927-D double eagle.

Dr. Charles Green Sale, B. Max Mehl, lot 917, April 1949 for $630 (we were not able to examine a photo of the Green coin).

This coin is identified by a series of marks in the left obverse field.

4. The F.C.C. Boyd specimen in "World's Greatest Collection," Numismatic Gallery, lot 1045, January 1946.

U.S. Gold Collection (Eliasberg) sold by Bowers and Ruddy, lot 1067, October 1982 for $170,000.

Sold by North American Certified Trading, January 2006 for "more than $1.9 million" to an anonymous East Coast dealer.

This coin is identified by marks on the lower fourth and fifth rays left from Liberty.

5. Lester Merkin Sale, lot 526, October 1969 for $32,000.

Gilhousen Collection Sale, Superior, lot 1041, February 1973 for $60,000.

This example is identified by "two marginally noticeable field marks, one belowforearm, the other midway branch and end border" (Merkin catalog, p. 39, and Superior catalog, p. 53).

6. Western Collection of U.S. Gold Coins, Stack's, lot 1252, December 1981 for $220,000.

King of Siam Collection, Bowers and Merena, lot 2201, October 1987 for $242,000.

Charles Kramer Collection of United States Gold Coins, Stack's/Superior, lot 913, November 1988 for $187,000.

Century Collection Sale, Superior, lot 3339, February 1982, did not sell.

January-February Sale, Superior, lot 1595, January-February 1993 for $137,500.

This specimen is identified by a field mark located midway between the end of Liberty's flowing hair and above rays 5-6 from left of her body, and by marks in the upper middle part of the eagle's left wing.

7. Auction '84 Sale, Paramount, lot 999, July 1984 for $198,000.

Dr. Thaine B. Price Collection, David Akers, lot 115, May 1998 for $577,500.

This piece is identified by marks on the upper middle part of ray 5 left from Liberty's body, by field marks between the upper middle parts of rays 6-9, and field marks between the upper parts of rays 2-5 on the lower right obverse.

8. Museum of Connecticut History specimen, Heritage, lot 6026, June 1995 for $390,500. Purchased by Jay Parrino.

This example is identified by marks above each of Liberty's knees, two marks on the upper middle ray left (facing) of her body, a mark on the lower third and fourth rays above the Capitol dome, and a series of marks above OD and W in GOD WE.

In our cataloging of the MCH piece, we stated: "To our knowledge this is the first unrecorded 1927-D twenty to appear at public auction in many years. The circumstances surrounding the appearance of this coin are quite curious, and unfortunately do not shed much light on why this piece was unknown to the numismatic community. It was purchased at the time of issue with another piece by the numismatic curator of the Museum of Connecticut History. Both pieces have been there since 1927. The mystery is why no one knew of their existence until now and why they were not included on the roster of known specimens that has been endlessly repeated each time a specimen has appeared over the past twenty years. Walter Breen did research in the MCH...but the '27-D twenties somehow escaped his attention."

Eric von Klinger, in the above-referenced *Coin World* article, elaborates further on the two 1927-D's in the Museum of Connecticut History Collection in a January 16, 2006 *Coin World* article: "David Nelson, administrator of the museum division, explained that State Librarian George Goddard had bought coins directly from the Mint each year of the 36 years (1900-1936) he was in that position. Goddard had gained favored access to Mint officials through Joseph C. Mitchelson, who bequeathed his coin holdings to the museum upon his death in 1911."

9. The second Museum of Connecticut History specimen, presently in the museum's collection.

10. Dallas Bank Collection (Jeff Browning), Sotheby's/Stack's, lot 206, October 2001 for $402,500.

Sold by Rare Coin Wholesalers to Legend Numismatics, June 2005 for $1.65 million.

This piece is identified by a mark on Liberty's left (right facing) ankle, and by marks on the middle part of rays 6 and 7 above the 19 in the date.

11. From the Charlotte et al. collections, Stack's, lot 1217, March 1991 for $479,750.

Philip Morse Collection, Heritage, lot 6697, November 2005 for $1,897,500.

This specimen is identified by a mark on Liberty's right (left facing) knee, and by a mark on each of the top portions of the 5th and 6th rays to the right (left facing) of her body.

12. Primary Bartle Collection of U.S. Gold Coins, Stack's, lot 868, October 1985 for $275,000.

Orlando Sale, Superior, lot 686, August 1992, did not sell.

Florida United Numismatists Sale, Heritage, lot 3624, January 2006 for $1,322,500. The coin was in an "old" NGC holder, conservatively graded over 10 years ago as MS65.

The specimen offered in this sale.

This coin is identified by a mark on the lower middle part of ray 4 on the left (right facing) side of Liberty, by a mark on the middle of ray 3 and another in the middle of ray 4 of the lower left obverse, and by marks on the middle of the left wing, and a mark on the tip of the feather above the tail feathers.

Most of the 1927-D double eagle appearances listed below have been included in previous rosters of extant specimens. Some of these coins may be duplicates of those listed above, while others may be separate examples. We list these apart from the above, as we did not have ready access to the catalogs that contained photos of the appearances, thus precluding a comparative analysis, or, the photos may have been of such quality that a definitive assessment could not be conducted.

A. The third Smithsonian specimen. According to the roster presented by Sotheby's/Stack's in their catalog of the Dallas Bank Collection Sale, October 2001, this specimen pedigrees to: "Lilly Estate (1968); Josiah K. Lilly Collection; Stack's; Robert Schermerhorn Collection; Dr. Charles Green Collection, Max Mehl, April 1949, lot 917; J.F. Bell Collection, Stack's, December 1944, lot 1004 (also see entry B next).

B. The Schermerhorn specimen, sold by Stack's in a private treaty transaction to Josiah K. Lilly in 1953. In his January 2006 *Coin World* article, von Klinger wrote that this specimen is "now in the Smithsonian Institution."

C. The Schmandt Collection, Stack's, lot 1072, February 1957.

D. A specimen submitted to NGC for grading by an anonymous West Coast dealer at the New York Invitational Show. The July 13, 2005 posting on the NGC web site states of the MS66-graded piece: "This particular specimen has long-resided in private collection and had never before been seen by a professional grading service."

All known 1927-D twenties display great luster and color. The surfaces are typically frosty with rich orange-gold or green-gold coloration. Striking details are usually complete, save for the usual softness on the stars in the lower left obverse quadrant. Mint records indicate that four pairs of dies and two edge collars were used to coin 1927-D double eagles. Apparently most, but not all of the remaining examples were struck from the same die pairing that includes the following characteristics:

1. A barely visible hairline die break from star to star through the top of L in LIBERTY;

2. A thin die break extends from the tip of the base of the L through the I to the torch; and

3. A thin, almost vertical, slightly offset die break bisects the eagle's beak on the reverse.

Blazing luster enlivens both sides of the Premium Gem offered in this lot. The surfaces display the typical frosty finish and rich orange-gold color imbued with traces of light green. A powerful strike manifests itself in bold definition on Liberty's facial features, fingers, and toes, on the panes of the Capitol dome, and on the eagle's plumage. The few light marks scattered about are well within the parameters of the MS66 grade designation. As with most known 1927-D double eagles, this piece shows the typical cracks at the base of the L in LIBERTY through the I to the top part of the torch, a barely visible hairline-thin crack from star 13 through the next few stars to the top of the L in LIB-ERTY, and a thin crack that bisects the eagle's beak. This could be a once-in-a-lifetime opportunity to acquire what is one of the finest known examples of the legendary 1927-D double eagle. Population: 4 in 66, 1 finer (11/06).(#9187)

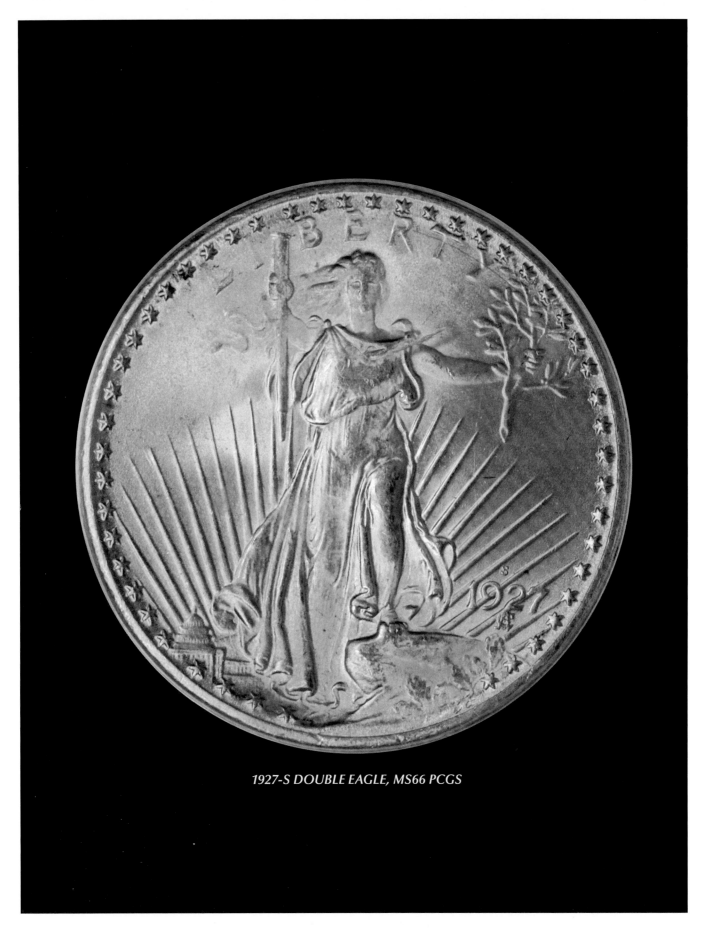

1927-S DOUBLE EAGLE, MS66 PCGS

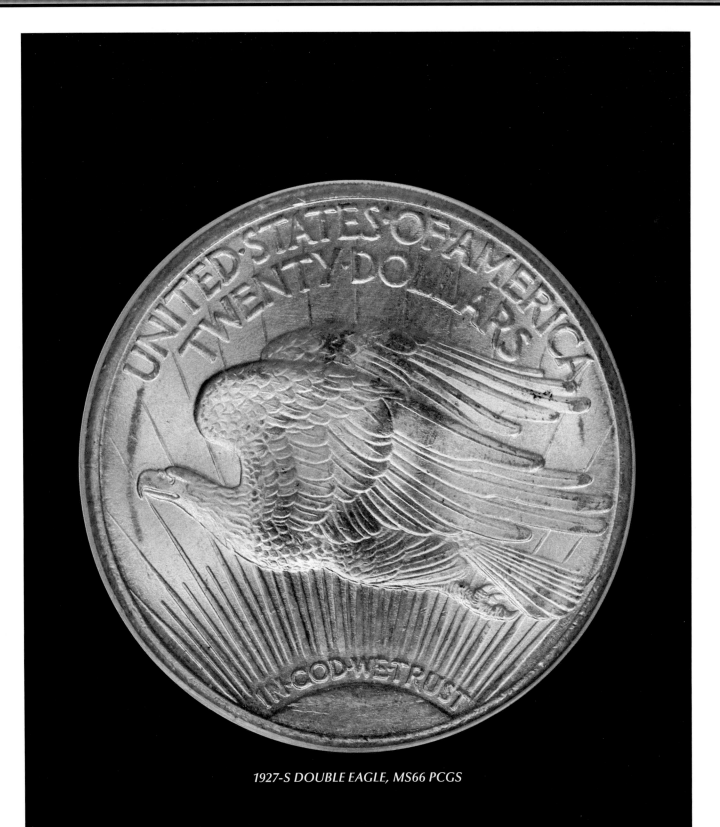

1927-S DOUBLE EAGLE, MS66 PCGS

Rare and Desirable 1927-S Premium Gem Double Eagle

3304   1927-S MS66 PCGS. The 1927-S double eagle stands out as one of the rarest and best-known issues of the Saint-Gaudens series, despite the fact that 3.1 million pieces were produced. The key status of the '27-S is based on absolute rarity rather than conditional rarity. PCGS and NGC have certified about 220 examples in all grades, some of which are undoubtedly resubmissions. David Akers, in his cataloging of the May 19, 1998 sale of the Dr. Thaine Price Collection, says: "The 1927-S double eagle is one of the most revered issues in the Saint-Gaudens double eagle series, and most known specimens are either high grade circulated examples or low grade Mint State pieces. Choice and Very Choice Uncirculated 1927-S double eagles are very rare and Gems are extremely rare. Looking back in history to the late 1940's and early 1950's, the 1927-S occupied an even more exalted position in the series than it does today. At that time, it was generally regarded as the fourth or fifth rarest issue in the series after the 1924-S, 1926-D and 1926-S, more or less on a par with the 1931-D. It was then considered to be even more rare than the 1927-D, which today is regarded as the premier issue in the series, as well as such now famous issues as 1920-S, 1921, 1930-S, 1931 and 1932. However, as was the case with many of the Saint-Gaudens issues that were thought to be ultra-rare, a small number of 1927-S double eagles trickled out of European banks over the next 20 years, although no really substantial quantities of this issue were ever found. Nevertheless, enough 'new' specimens came onto the market to reduce its overall rarity level from 'extremely rare', as was described by B. Max Mehl in the famous Dr. Charles W. Green sale in 1949, to the 'rare' status it holds today. In Gem condition, however, and especially in the superb condition represented by this specimen (the PCGS-graded MS66 coin in the Price sale), Mehl's earlier 'extremely rare' description of the 1927-S is still valid." The population data corroborate Akers' assessment of the rarity level of high-end Uncirculated examples of the 1927-S. Only 11 coins have been graded MS65, six specimens have been assigned MS66, and a mere three pieces rated MS67.

The presently-offered Premium Gem displays peach-gold patina that is accompanied on the obverse by tinges of light tan, and on the reverse by subtle yellow-green undertones and occasional splashes of orange color. Attractive luster radiates from both faces, and the motifs are well impressed. The Capitol building, which is typically weak on this issue, exhibits nice detail in most of the panes. Liberty's facial features, the fingers on both hands, the toes, and the eagle's plumage are all sharp. A solitary light copper spot in the lower left obverse field and a small mark in the middle of Liberty's outstretched left arm may help in the coin's pedigree. This outstanding piece is sure to generate spirited bidding among aficionados of rare-date Saint-Gaudens coinage, and clearly one of the highlights among the double eagles of the Kutasi Collection. Population: 2 in 66, 1 finer (11/06).
From The Kutasi Collection.(#9188)

Exquisite 1928 Superb Gem Twenty Dollar

3305   1928 MS67 PCGS. The 1928 has the largest mintage (8.8 million pieces) of any U.S. gold coin of any denomination. Consequently, it is the most common date in the Saint-Gaudens twenty dollar series after the 1924 and 1927. Only in MS67 does this issue present a challenge to the Saint-Gaudens double eagle enthusiast. The presently-offered Superb Gem displays an exquisite strike and thick mint frost. Lovely peach-gold color with light greenish tinges bathes highly lustrous surfaces that are free of annoying marks. An inoffensive linear mark above the outstretched arm of Liberty is mentioned as a possible pedigree marker. Population: 64 in 67, 0 finer (10/06).
From The Kutasi Collection.(#9189)

Vibrant 1929 Double Eagle, MS65

3306   1929 MS65 PCGS. Nearly 1.8 million double eagles were coined in 1929, all at the Philadelphia Mint. All issues from this date on are great rarities, with the 1929 being most obtainable with respect to overall availability. Gold specialist David Akers (1998) writes: "...Of the final five collectible issues of the Saint-Gaudens series, the 1929 is, by a substantial margin, the most 'common' in terms of population rarity since specimens below Gem quality can be obtained with only moderate difficulty. This is especially true in the past few years since a number of newly discovered specimens have recently come onto the market, some of which are quite nice, grading Choice and Very Choice Uncirculated. However, true Gems of this issue ...are still very rare, if not extremely rare, at least on a par with the more highly regarded 1931 and 1932."

Estimates of 1929 survivors range from 60 examples, that Breen (1988) calls "reasonable," to a few hundred, which he says is "most likely too high." David Bowers (2004) suggests that up to 1,750 pieces are extant. The latter estimate is not in line with current population statistics, that reveal fewer than 300 certified examples. It does not seem likely that a sizeable quantity of an expensive coin such as the 1929 twenty dollar could exist without a substantial number being certified.

The 1929 Gem in this lot displays vibrant luster with peach-gold patina and a few splashes of slightly deeper orange color. A powerful strike emboldens the design elements, that exhibit crisp delineation on the Capitol building, on Liberty's face, fingers, and toes, on the olive branch, and on the eagle's feathers. Both sides are remarkably well preserved and clean, much more so than what might be expected for the grade level. A small linear mark just preceding the left wing to the left of the first T in TWENTY helps to pedigree the coin. Population: 19 in 65, 5 finer (11/06).
From The Kutasi Collection.(#9190)

Rare and Outstanding 1930-S Double Eagle

3307   1930-S MS66 PCGS. Ex: Price. Apparently, all but a few handfuls of the 74,000-piece mintage of 1930-S double eagles were melted, with the surviving coins probably obtained directly from the Mint in 1930. Walter Breen, in his *Encyclopedia of U.S. and Colonial Coins,* asserts that: "Possibly 25 survive, almost all Unc. with bag marks; most came from European banks about 1960." David Akers, in his 1998 catalog of the Dr. Thaine Price Collection, estimates 50 to 60 pieces to be extant (see below). This latter estimate is in line with PCGS/NGC population figures, that show slightly more than 50 certified coins that reveal a modal grade of MS64.

Akers sheds light on the 1930-S double eagle rarity level in the Price catalog: "...the 1930-S is one of the greatest rarities in this ever popular series. Since virtually all of the relatively few known specimens are mint state, it is obvious that this issue never saw actual circulation, and it is more than likely that the entire mintage (74,000 pieces, very small by Saint-Gaudens standards) was melted. The specimens that exist today were, in all probability, obtained by collectors or visitors directly from the Mint in the year of issue. In terms of the total number of specimens known, there are undoubtedly fewer 1930-S double eagles than there are examples of any collectible regular issue in this series other than the 1927-D. In other words, all grades considered, there are more examples of the 1920-S, 1921, 1927-S, 1931, 1931-D, and 1932 around than there are examples of the 1930-S. This is in contrast to its relative rarity ranking of 50 years ago when the 1930-S was considered to be only the fourth rarest S Mint issue of the series after the 1924-S, 1926-S and 1927-S. It was also felt to be significantly less rare than the 1926-D, 1921, and the 1931-D. It is difficult to say for sure, but the total number of 1930-S double eagles known is probably in the range of only 50-60 pieces. Some are quite nice with Choice and Very Choice Uncirculated being perhaps the most typically encountered grades, but true Gems...are of extreme rarity with no more than 6-8 such examples known."

The 1930-S we offer in this sale comes out of the above-mentioned Thaine Price Collection. We quote some of Akers' remarks in his cataloging of the Price specimen (lot 119): "This is a fabulous coin, at least equal to any I have ever seen, maybe even the finest, with its only rivals being the gorgeous Gem from Stack's March 1991 sale, lot 1221, and the coin from the Museum of Connecticut History sold by Heritage as lot 6031 in June 1995...The surfaces...have just a very slight natural haze, a hallmark of the coin's originality and the fact that it has never been cleaned, dipped or otherwise tampered with in anyway...When I purchased this coin for Dr. Price in the late 1980's, it had been off the market for more than 40 years. I...showed it to several dealer friends who are experts in this series, and their reaction was uniformly one of amazement at the beauty and phenomenal quality of the coin; all agreed that they had never seen another 1930-S double eagle quite like it."

To Akers' fitting overview of this wonderful Premium Gem, we add the following. Both faces are enlivened with dazzling luster that radiates from richly colored orange-gold surfaces that are interspersed, especially on the reverse, with splashes of mint-green. A well executed strike has resulted in crisp definition on the intricately-designed panes on the Capitol building, on Liberty's face, fingers, and toes, on the olive branch, and on the eagle's plumage. All in all, an outstanding example of this classic rarity. Population: 5 in 66, 0 finer (11/06). *From The Kutasi Collection.*(#9191)

Rare 1931 Premium Gem Double Eagle

3308   1931 MS66 PCGS. The 1931 Philadelphia Mint double eagle is very rare today, and is one of the key issues in the series. Walter Breen, in his *Encyclopedia of U.S. and Colonial Coins,* suggests that: "Possibly 18-20 survive, all Unc." PCGS and NGC, however, have seen approximately 120 examples, all but two of which are in Mint State grades. In his writeup of the Gem Uncirculated 1931 specimen in the Dr. Thaine B. Price sale (May 1998), David Akers says: "For many years, the 1931 was considered to be the second most common of the rare late date issues of the Saint-Gaudens series, i.e., those issues from 1929-1932. It was considered to be more rare than the 1929, but less rare than the other three, in particular, the 1932. This always struck me as odd because in-depth research clearly showed the 1931 to be at least as rare as the 1932 in terms of the total number of specimens known, and perhaps even a little bit more rare. That misconception has been corrected now, and today the 1931 is appropriately regarded as the second rarest of the late date issues with respect to population rarity after only the 1930-S. In Gem condition, however, the 1931 is the most common of the issues from 1929-1932 (just slightly less rare than the 1932, but considerably less rare than the 1930-S and 1931-D as well as the 1929), although most standard pricing guides do not properly reflect that fact."

The modal Uncirculated grade in the certified population for the 1931 twenty is MS64, with nearly 50 specimens having been seen. Thirty-five Gems have been graded, and nearly 15 MS66 examples. A solitary finer coin has been certified (a PCGS-graded MS67). It is instructive to note that, according to our records, 22 MS65 1931 examples have appeared in major auctions over the last 15 years, but only three MS66s and one MS67.

The 1931, according to Akers (*A Handbook of 20-Century United States Gold Coins*), is usually well struck, although some examples are rather flat in the stars below the Capitol building. The surfaces display excellent mint frost, and the color is usually light to medium orange or coppery-gold. Copper alloy spots are commonly seen, and some specimens display a long, vertical, slightly curved die break through the eagle's beak.

The Premium Gem in the present lot exhibits somewhat better-than-average strike, as the detail in the Capitol building and the eagle's plumage is sharp, and most of the stars along the lower obverse border are well brought up. Rich orange-gold patina intermingles with yellow-gold and tinges of mint-green, and pleasing luster emanates from satiny-like surfaces that are devoid of significant abrasions. A few minute marks beneath the ends of Liberty's flowing hair and a couple more below the olive branch may aid in this coin's pedigree. This example does not show any copper spots, or the die crack through the eagle's beak. Population: 9 in 66, 1 finer (11/06).
From The Kutasi Collection.(#9192)

Rare 1931-D MS66 Double Eagle, Among the Finest Known

3309 **1931-D MS66 PCGS.** Ex: Price. During the sparse-coinage year of 1931, in the midst of the Great Depression, only 106,500 double eagles were produced at the Denver Mint. These were struck primarily for export, but except for a few, it appears that most never left the Treasury vaults, and were eventually melted in the late 1930s. Concerning the rarity status of the 1931, David Akers (May 19, 1998) writes: "In the distant past, the 1931-D was widely regarded as the fourth or fifth rarest issue of the Saint-Gaudens double eagle series, surpassed in rarity only by the 1924-S, 1926-D and 1926-S, as well as possibly the 1927-S, although the latter was usually considered about the equal of the 1931-D. The 1927-D, now the premier issue of the series, was actually thought to be less rare than this issue until the early 1950s when small quantities of the 1931-D first began showing up in European banks. Over the next two decades, several mini-hoards of the 1931-D were discovered, but relatively few of these pieces graded better than Choice Uncirculated and the majority were heavily marked and lackluster."

PCGS and NGC have certified, to date, 145 1931-D double eagles, only three of which are not in Uncirculated grades. The vast majority of 1931-Ds seen by the services (107 pieces) fall into the MS62 to MS64 range. Twenty-three Gems have been graded, and a mere four MS66 coins. None finer have been seen by either service. Auction records are in concert with the population data. Perusal of Krause Publications' *Auction Prices Realized,* along with our own auction records, indicates that Gem and finer appearances of the 1931-D are scant. Ten MS65 pieces have gone through the major auction houses in the past 15 or so years, and only one MS66.

The Premium Gem 1931-D specimen offered in this lot comes out of the Dr. Thaine B. Price Collection, and was previously off the market for 40 years. Akers, in his catalog description of the Price coin, writes: "... one of the two finest examples of this very rare issue that I have seen, possibly even the finest. The only other example that has any real claim to matching it is the superb Amon Carter specimen (now in the Dr. Steven Duckor Collection), which is the only 1931-D graded MS66 by any major grading service as of the writing of this catalog. This Dr. Price specimen, however, has even cleaner surfaces than the Duckor-Carter specimen, and it equals it in terms of its eye appeal and overall appearance. The color of this coin is an ultra-rich orange gold and, like the Duckor-Carter coin, the luster is extraordinary, something not at all typical of this issue which is generally the least attractive of the late dates from 1929 to 1932. There is one small mark in the field between Liberty's outstretched arm and TY, and there are also a few other tiny marks, as well as a couple of faint hairlines, but by the strictest standards, this is a Gem of the highest order and is actually one of the choicest coins in Dr. Price's entire collection of Saint-Gaudens double eagles." To Akers' description of this outstanding 1931-D, we add the following. Blushes of mint-green, yellow-gold, and lavender accent the orange-gold patina, and potent luster enlivens both sides. A well executed strike manifests itself in sharp definition on Liberty's head, hands, and foot, as well as on the panes of the Capitol building and the eagle's feathers. Connoisseurs of Saint-Gaudens gold coinage will not want to miss out on the chance to acquire one of the finest known representatives of this rare date. Population: 2 in 66, 0 finer (11/06).
From The Kutasi Collection.(#9193)

Desirable 1932 Premium Gem Twenty Dollar

3310   1932 MS66 PCGS. The 1932, representing the last readily collectible Saint-Gaudens double eagle, is one of the most desired issues in the series. Estimates vary on the number of survivors out of the original 1,101,750-piece mintage. Walter Breen writes in the *Complete Encyclopedia of U.S. and Colonial Coins,* that possibly 22 to 25 examples exist, almost all of which are Uncirculated. David Bowers, in the *Guide Book of Double Eagle Gold Coins,* estimates that between 60 to 80 coins are extant. David Akers, in his cataloging of the Gem Uncirculated 1932 twenty dollar gold piece from the Dr. Thaine Price Collection, gives a similar estimate of surviving examples (see below).

Akers presents an in-depth assessment of the rarity status of the 1932 double eagle. "...A number of years ago, it was, for some reason, fashionable to consider the 1932 double eagle the rarest of the late date Saint-Gaudens double eagles, and the 1932 often sold for a significant premium over the prices realized by the other issues. That situation has been corrected, however, and now it is generally agreed that the 1932 is more rare in terms of the total number of specimens known than only the 1929 and 1931-D. There are certainly fewer 1930-S double eagles in existence than there are 1932, and the 1931 also seems to be a little more scarce than the 1932 in terms of population rarity. With respect to *condition rarity,* however, the situation is a little different. The 1932 is slightly more rare than the 1931 in Gem Uncirculated condition, but less rare than the 1931-D and even the 1929. (The 1930-S is the uncontested late date champion in terms of both population rarity and condition rarity.) Perhaps as many as 70-80 examples are known of this issue. Most are quite nice and many of them grade Very Choice Uncirculated, or at least Choice Uncirculated. True Gems, however, are very rare with approximately 13-16 pieces known."

Of the 125 1932 specimens that have been seen by PCGS and NGC to date, all are in Mint State, particularly in MS64 and MS65 (77 pieces). Nineteen coins have been certified MS66, and none finer. The frequency of appearance of 1932 double eagles at auction more or less reflects the PCGS/NGC population data. MS64 and MS65 pieces have made slightly over 30 appearances within the last 15 years, while MS66-graded specimens have appeared eight times over the same time period.

A potent strike on the current MS66 specimen is manifested in crisp definition on Liberty's facial features and fingers, and on the eagle's plumage. Frosty surfaces display attractive hues of greenish-gold highlighted with an occasional splash of orange, and radiate pleasing luster. There are no contact marks worthy of individual mention. A small toning spot on the lower left obverse between the eighth and ninth rays that are located close to the gown may help in identification of the coin. Population: 7 in 66, 0 finer (11/06).
From The Kutasi Collection.(#9194)